The Ups and Downs of J.C.

"MY CRAZY LIFE"
"MI VIDA LOCA"

JORGE A. CAMACHO

Copyright © 2025 by Jorge A. Camacho

All rights reserved. Except as permitted under the U.S. Copyright Act of 1976, no part of this publication may be reproduced, distributed, or transmitted in any form or by any means, or stored in a database or retrieval system, without the prior written permission of the publisher.

HIS Publishing Group
12426 Pleasant Valley Drive
Dallas, TX 75243

All Scripture is from the Holy Bible, New International Version®, NIV® unless otherwise noted. Copyright ©1973, 1978, 1984, 2011 by Biblica, Inc.® Used by permission. All rights reserved worldwide.

Printed in the United States of America

Hardback - 979-8-9926528-1-9
Soft cover - 979-8-9926528-0-2
eBook - 979-8-9926528-2-6

Division of Human Improvement Specialists, llc.
www.hispubg.com | info@hispubg.com

CONTENTS

Dedication 5
Acknowledgment 7
Introduction 9

Life In Mexico 11
Texas Bound 23
Pleasant Grove Back To Dallas 29
The First Time 37
Paint In The City 41
Stephen C. Foster And Beyond 53
My First Job 71
The Journey Continues 79
Old Ways 95
Toxic Females 107
Total Denial 129
No More Tears 139
My Last Rodeo 147
The North Tower 153
Deep Dreams 167
The Master 191
The Long Road Back 213

My Journey Of Life Continued	217
The Roller Coaster Chain	223
Horseshoes	229
Living Life In The Pods	235
Working The Program	255
Revival	263
Life Is A Ministry	271
Dream On	279
Too Good To Be True	283
Ready For The Free World	285
9/11/2001	287
The Walls Unit Again?	293
Convictions	297
Free At Last	303
Store #3585	311
The Corporate Life	315
Plain Crazy	319
Old Jerry	325
Opportunities	327
Covid-19	341
Live Oak	361
My Wonderful Father	377
My Memories Of Lifes Ups And Downs And Some Pleasures	385
Surgery At The Hospital	425
Giving Thanks For All Things	435
In Closing	455
Miscellaneous Photos	457

DEDICATION

To my wonderful parents Jesus O.
Camacho and Rosa S. Camacho.

To my Baby Pie of The World, Justin Adam Camacho.
Even though I did not witness your birth, I have been
blessed to be in your life from first grade through your
graduation from high school and beyond. I will always
be there for you for the rest of my life . May God Bless
you, my precious son; you will always be my life.

To my sisters Elsa, Alma, and Mary for supporting
and standing by my side in the most challenging time
of my life. And caring for my precious son.

To my brothers, Beto and Pepe, for helping the family and me
when we needed it the most, especially while I was away.

To my extended family who put up with all my
wrongdoings and never stopped loving me.

ACKNOWLEDGMENT

To my dear family,

I have put my story in writing to acknowledge all the pain and suffering I have put you through. I want to apologize sincerely for all my wrongdoing. I am especially sorry to Mother and Father for not listening to you or taking your advice. You did your best to make me understand and were always there for me.

I love you all.

INTRODUCTION

IN THE BEGINNING

Once upon a time, a little child lived in Valle Hermoso Tamaulipas, Mexico, where he played in a pile of dirt topped with burnt ashes. He was playing with a broken piece of scrap metal plate, which was his toy at the time. Not knowing any better, he continued to play in the dirt until his mother came out of the house and spanked him for playing in such a dangerous place. That little child was Jorge A. Camacho, the third child to his parents, Jesus O. and Rosa Sosa Camacho.

I really do not know how to start this story. It has a lot of ups and downs. My life was fun at one point and another; however, I would eventually face a lot of problems in my future. The dates and places may not be accurate.

Rosa Sosa Camacho at age twenty-two

I was around four or five years old and was being raised by my two aunts and some uncles.

My two Uncles and Tia Amelia

LIFE IN MEXICO

My mother, Rosa, was wonderful and was always there for me. She traveled back and forth across the border with my father, Jesus, who was born in Gregory, Texas. One summer, I remember living in our house in Valle Hermoso, Mexico. My older brother Beto and I had some baby pet birds and doves. Every morning, we couldn't wait to go out and feed them. I remember wanting to be first and doing everything myself so I would get all the attention.

My older sister Elsa would scold me for being rude and not respecting my siblings. If I disobeyed her, I would be spanked for not listening to her. My dad lived at our house part of the time because he was working in Tejas (Texas), where I would soon end up. Dad would come and go; sometimes on his trips home, I did not see him at all. He returned only when he was on vacation or during holidays. He would make sure things were right with all of us and would take care of his other responsibilities. He owned land with crops, many horses, and cattle. The cattle produced milk that he sold weekly to a local milk company. My dad had people working for him, but he wanted to make sure the operation was under control.

Jesus O. Camacho at age thirty-eight   *Jesus O. Camacho at age twenty-six*

I remember how he used to tell me to keep a look out and let him know if I saw any trucks coming in the distance. He would add water to the barrels of milk and end up with four extra barrels of milk. My dad was a clever man. More milk meant more money. He was just doing what he thought was right at the time to earn extra money for his family, whom he loved very much. He wanted to make sure we were taken care of. What a wonderful and amazing man.

There were five of us at the time. My older sister, my older brother Beto, myself, my younger brother Pepe, and my little sister Alma. I constantly fought with my brothers over everything. We were all sent to school to get an education, but I was unbelievably bad, and the things I did made no sense. My teacher would make me sit at her desk and draw these so-called circles all the time.

I did not like going to school because every kid there hated us for some reason. They were always picking on Beto and threatening to hurt us after school. Also, every day when we got out of school there was this crazy man we called "Crazy Abel." He would block the path we took to get home and expected us to give him a snack or candy bar before we could pass. When you are young, little, and scared, you believe the stories people tell you. Well, we believed everything about how crazy he was, so we made sure to have a snack or candy bar to give him. After all, to us he really looked and acted like a crazy person. We would come to know him better later in life.

Chuy & His Family

I skipped school at times, and when I got caught, my uncles scolded me or told me that if I didn't go to school, I would not get my allowance. My father sent $1.00 U.S. money for each of us kids. To us, to have twelve and a half silver pesos in Mexican money was a lot of money. I tried to save as much as possible because the coins were magical and beautiful with an eagle holding a snake on one side. I bought lots of candy, marbles, and string tops, which were fun to play with at school. I always lost my marbles, and my tops split in half. It seemed that I had friends when I had money, but when I did not have money, those so-called friends were my enemies. I could never understand or figure out why they would turn on me.

I attended school for only a brief time and when I wasn't in school, I wandered here and there. I regret not staying in school and learning so I could become a better and more responsible person. My father wanted me to have a successful future. Today, I can't write Spanish. Mother really wanted all of us to attend schools in Texas because she believed the U.S. was the land of opportunity. My dad wanted us to attend Mexican schools.

There are good memories from our time on the ranch at Valle Hermoso, like the time I had a little bull as a pet. Dad would throw me on top of that bull, and the bull would get angry and kick when I rode him. I remember learning to swim. Dad would throw me into a big pond over and over until I started swimming. Boy, I was so scared that I learned fast so I wouldn't drown. I was determined to get out of that water as soon as possible.

DANGER AT THE FARMHOUSE

Nineteen sixty-six was one of my best years ever. That summer everything was beautiful. The land was green and lush with thick stalks of corn and lots of sorghum in the fields. I will never forget that summer.

Sorghum fields

Our land in Mexico

Preparing the land for planting

However, heavy thunderstorms rolled in, and it rained like crazy every day for weeks. Things were bad, and warnings were all around. One day, a tornado came through town that caused the land to flood. I remember that day, just like it was yesterday. I wanted to roam around, and the water came up to my chest. There were places where the water was too deep to walk. The water caused a lot of damage to the corn and sorghum fields.

Corn fields

My dad grabbed a blue tarp and using ropes covered his 1946 black truck. I don't remember if the truck was a GMC or Ford, but he loved that truck. That is when he said, "Enough is enough." I could have sworn I also heard him telling my mother that we were moving to Texas. He wasn't about to have us go through another flood. They were too dangerous, and he didn't want to risk anything. The move took some time, a year or less.

I lived at the farmhouse with my two aunts and uncles for a few years. I am so proud of my aunt, Tia Amelia. She was like our second mother, always caring for us and treating us like her own. My other aunt, Tia Lupe, was a little younger, but she did a lot for us as well. They both worked hard making meals, cleaning the house, and doing laundry. They made sure we were taken care of. My uncles took us to town on weekends to get haircuts and buy supplies, and sometimes they would take us to the movies, which was fun.

My grandfather, Jose Sosa, also lived with us and was such a unique person. I looked up to him and admired him. Behaviorists claim that people start taking responsibility for themselves by watching the example set by others. I really believe in that theory, and it makes sense in many ways. Grandfather Sosa instilled a strong work ethic in each of us, and that ethic is the reason today we are a working family.

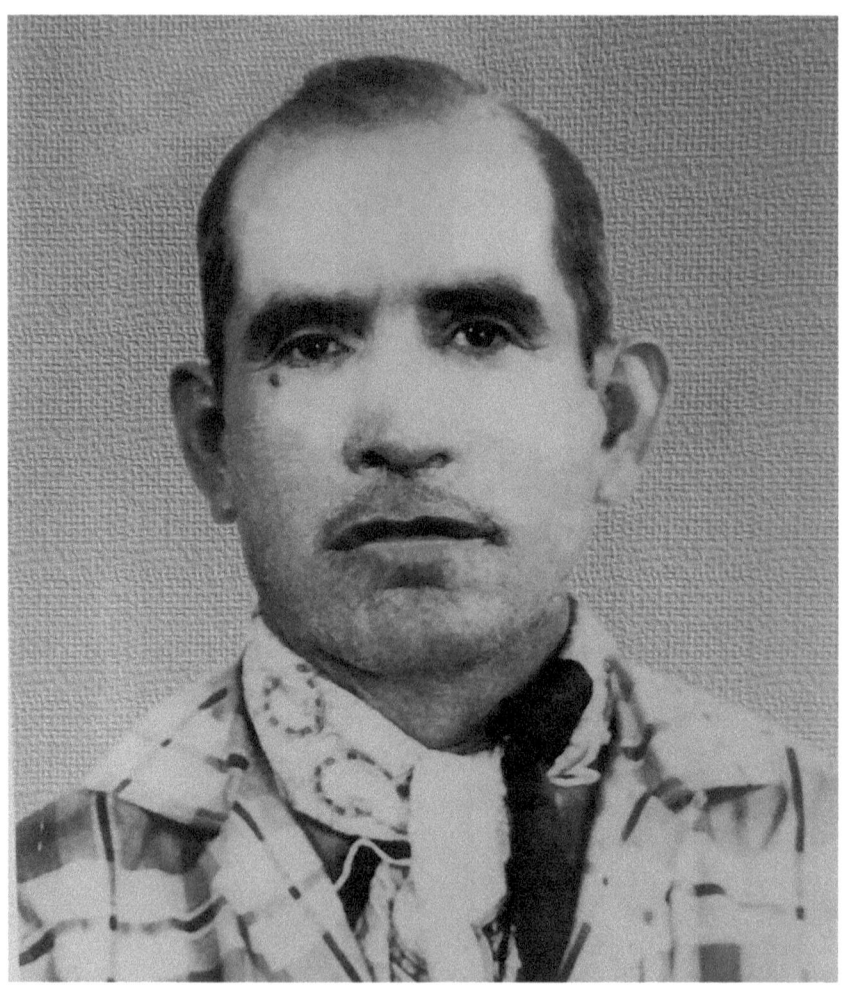

My Grand Father Jose Sosa

One crazy summer, several events happened. First my little sister Alma, who was about two or three years of age, drank some kind of fluid that had been left out on the front porch. Well, the liquid was toxic, and she was immediately rushed to the doctor's office. Scared the heck out of my mother, and for days she cried and got very emotional. In fact, we were all scared. I could not understand why anyone would leave a toxic fluid lying around.

Alma must have thought it was water or soda pop. She learned a valuable lesson.

Then, one of our dogs came down with rabies and started foaming from his mouth. The dog tried to bite us kids several times and was acting wild and crazy. We had no choice but to put him down.

The following week, my father and my aunt struggled with a six-foot snake that was big and scary looking. At the far end of the barn a snake had been eating our baby chickens and the eggs in their cages. I remember our dogs chasing the snake and attacking it in hopes of killing it, but they were unsuccessful. They were great dogs and were always protecting our land, house, and everyone who lived there. My father and my aunt tied a machete to the end of a long pole using string and tape. They made sure the blade was tied well and then poked at the snake and stabbed it several times, but the snake wouldn't die. In fact, it appeared strong and not fazed by their attacks and slithered under the house.

The house was built strongly and was set off from the ground about three feet to keep the water out. The floor of the house was made from two by four boards. I remember looking down through some of the cracks and seeing the snake. It was staring up at me with its tongue sticking out and was very ugly and evil looking. I got scared and ran to my room.

Eventually, my father, aunt, and the dogs managed to get the job done. After removing the snake from under the house they stretched it from one end to the other across the road. Dad measured the snake to be six feet long and then hung it on a tree near the road. It has been said that after you kill a large snake and hang it on a tree, it would rain. Later my dad said, "After I hung that snake it rained like crazy." But I don't remember any rain, so he might have been joking.

Soon after my father left us again. I can still hear him say, "I'm just going to the other side." I climbed to the top of the channel that separated some of the cornfields to look in hopes of seeing where he might be going. But all I saw were fields of corn and sorghum. Like I said before, weeks, or even months might pass before dad came back.

I continued to help my grandfather and uncles care for our crops. I was more in their way than being of any help considering I was just a little kid. They depended heavily on the rain to fill channel ditches, which were used to water the crops. When there was a lot of rain, there would be a good harvest, and, of course, more money earned, which was always good.

However, when there was little or no rain, life got rough, and sacrifices had to be made. We bought only things needed to get by. The fear that the cattle could starve because there would not be enough grass for them to feed haunted us. When this happened, we had to sell the cattle early, and that meant less money.

Around Christmas one year, my dad returned and brought all of us toys and other presents. We all had an exciting reunion. I always told him what I wanted for Christmas, a bike, and he got it for me. However, before he could give me the bike, my cousin Simon Martinez stole it out of my dad's truck and started riding around. Simon told us that he had ridden the bike all the way from Dallas to where we were living and we all believed him.

I remember going to town with my dad alone in his 1951 pickup truck. He made me whistle and yell, "Hey good looking" or "Hey beautiful" whenever we passed young ladies. Then, he would just smile and say, "Way to go, son." I liked that it was just the two of us together, father and son. How exciting those times were.

It was summer, and he had made enough money to get us all processed and legally across the border. But before we were to leave Mexico, he wanted to make one final stop. He took us all to Monterrey, Mexico, where we stayed in a hotel for about a week. Monterrey was an exceptionally large and beautiful city, with lots of nice friendly people from all cultures. I remember looking out the window of our hotel at the beautiful mountains.

On another night, I noticed a fire across the street. The fire was getting bigger and bigger, and I started to panic and ran for cover. My dad told us to stay put and not to worry. The fire fighters struggled for hours but eventually were able to put out the fire. Dad was always calm and in control.

It was an amazing time for me.

I was excited to see my dad but at the same time was curious about what he was up to. Little did we know he had been saving, wanting to buy us a new home in Dallas, Texas. He started to sell his cattle, horses, and some of the land he owned. We all enjoyed having him around because he would take us to town to eat and buy us toys and other things.

Ranch horses

TEXAS BOUND

After a wonderful vacation, we were on our way to Dallas, Texas. We arrived at Grandmother's house. My father's mother, Juanita Camacho Olvera, is an extremely sweet, caring person. We stayed with her for a few months until my dad had saved up enough money for a down payment on a house he found in Pleasant Grove.

My cousin Simon Marinez was also staying at grandmother's house and was constantly getting me in trouble. Simon was wild and crazy. He would tell my parents that I was going to sleep over in his room, but later told me he changed his mind. He would make me stay up late and beat me up. Once he tried to do a trick and threw me up in the air, I landed awkwardly and broke my right arm, which had to be put in a cast. My parents were so upset and spanked me for listening to him. He was a troublemaker.

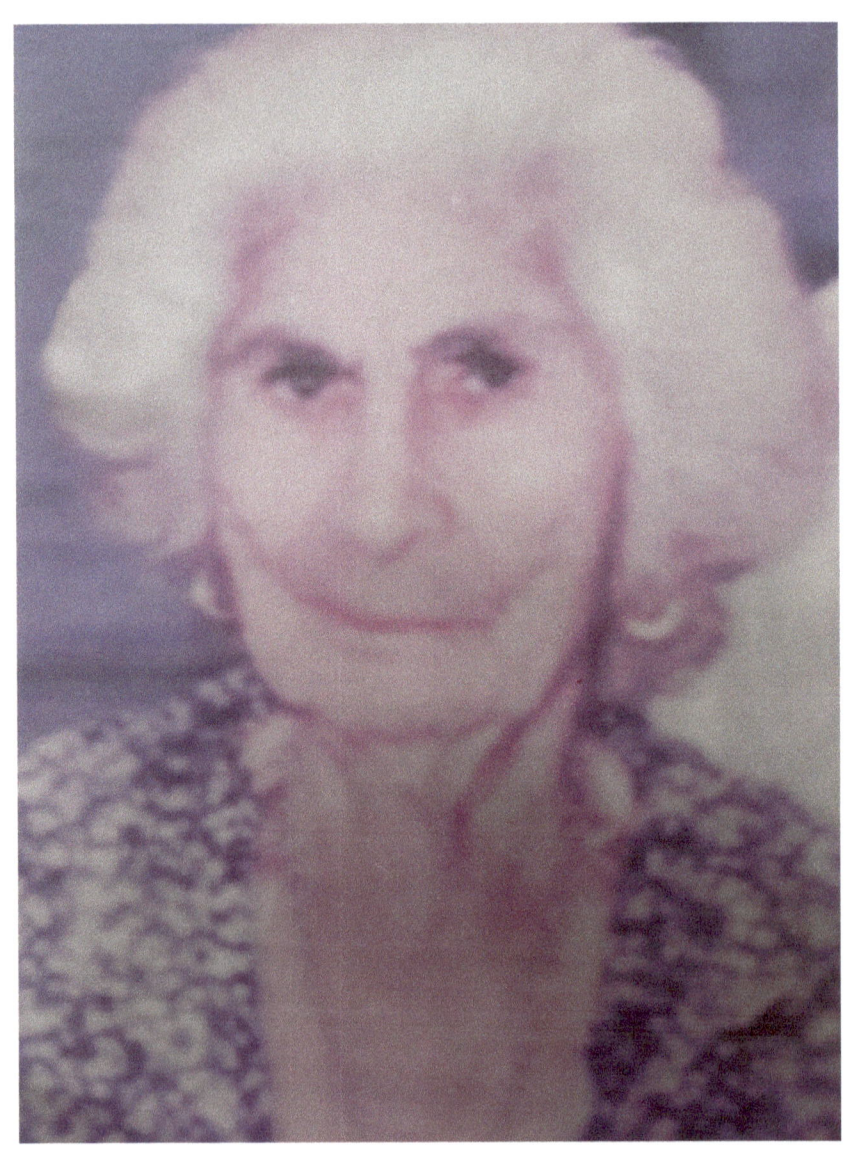

Grand Mother Juanita O. Camacho

FIRST SCHOOL

Dad finished raising the money, finalized the paperwork, and was able to purchase the home in Pleasant Grove. We would be living close to some of our relatives, and these were much better cousins. We had a good relationship with them even though we had a few scuffles at times. But that's just part of growing up and being a kid.

W.A. Blair Elementary School

I attended W.A. Blair Elementary School where they started me in kindergarten. However, before I knew it, I was promoted to first grade and then second grade. I remember the teacher taking roll and calling out my name, "Jorge," and some of the kids laughed and made fun of me. Some of my classmates would twist it around and call me "hard head," and the rest of the class would laugh including myself. I was embarrassed at first, but I got used to it and went with the flow. I endured their abuse until one day my teacher started calling me "George." Everyone liked that name, and before long, they were all calling me George. That is how my nickname was born.

My first grade picture   *Father and Mother holding my little sister Mary E. Camacho*

I had this so-called girlfriend named Terri. She would come looking for me and always wanted to kiss me on the cheek. I would run from her like no tomorrow. She was extremely attractive, and we had lots of fun together. She often came over and watched television at my house. She always tried to get me to sit on her lap at school and when I was over at her house. Her family had this great, big, pretty house with a big swimming pool in the backyard. I liked to go over and go swimming.

She was not only beautiful but talented. She was a good tap dancer and would dance in front of me with her swimsuit on. Not only was she beautiful but she also had incredible blue eyes. If I had kept up with her, it is possible we would have married one day. Her parents liked me, and my mother really liked her. My mother always told me she looked like a baby doll.

Well, in school I hung around a friend named Scott. We played sports together, such as soccer, baseball, and basketball. We also attended weekly Boy Scout meetings. We had fun, and he was a devoted friend. Unfortunately, it was not long before I would have to leave my friends, Scott, Terri, the school, our relatives in Pleasant Grove, and the house at 7420 Neuhoff.

My parents decided to downgrade because my dad was the only person earning money. The cost of living was high, and he was struggling to pay the mortgage and put food on the table for all of us. His strategy was to look for something more affordable where he could save up a larger down payment and reduce the monthly mortgage payments. He didn't want to be faced with this issue again.

PLEASANT GROVE BACK TO DALLAS

My dad found a house to rent close to where my grandmother had lived for a couple of years, and we moved back to Dallas. One year later, we were able to move a block over into our own home at 3117 Story Lane.

I started attending David G. Burnett Elementary School where I would finish the remainder of my second year and third and fourth grades.

Three boys and three girls 1970

I got into many fights at school because I got tired of kids picking on me for no reason. Just because I was new to the school, they were always testing me. There were three individuals that I particularly struggled with: Timothy, Wayne, and Chuck. They were all different builds, and each had a unique fighting style.

Timothy was short and fast and gave me the most trouble. He was tough to beat and occasionally got the best of me. He was in great shape and knew how to fight and defend himself.

Wayne, on the other hand, was a combination fighter and wrestler. He would try to pin me down with his wrestling skills and then finish me off. He was the second-best fighter and gave me trouble, but we were about even.

Chuck was a beast. I never could beat him. He was big and heavy set and a bully. He would scratch, bite, and claw his way out of a fight. I fought him once, and he almost choked me to death. Another time, he was beating on me, but my big brother came to the rescue and ran him off.

I liked our house on Story Lane because of all the activity and action going on all the freaking time, especially on weekends. It was a wild and crazy street. The main leader of the gang called The Scorpions lived across the street. Next door to him was a band that played Spanish music. They held rehearsals, practiced on weekends, and attracted a lot of people,

THE GOOD TIMES

Story Lane had a curve on one end and there was a field on that side. There we played baseball and had soccer games. I witnessed a lot of accidents on the street, especially on weekends. People would get drunk and veer off the road or run into a telephone pole.

Of course, there were all of we guys and girls running around, riding bikes, and jumping ramps. It was an exciting time for me growing up, and I really enjoyed this era of my life. Kids would come from other neighborhoods to play against us, each side hoping to gain bragging rights. On some summer nights, we went to the movies at the drive-in in the parking lot of Texas Stadium, home of The Dallas Cowboys, America's Team!

Back then, they were tough to beat.

When we wanted to go to the movie, we loaded the car with food and drinks, and then all of us but the driver climbed into the trunk so we wouldn't have to pay. Back then the movie was only $1.00 or $2.00, depending on the day, and $3.00 dollars' worth of gas got us everywhere we wanted to go: Lake Dallas, Grapevine Lake, and North Lake. Living in Dallas, Texas. We called those the Good Ole Times.

Keta Jacoba and Anna Lopez

Texas Stadium

I also had this so-called girlfriend at the time named Anna. She was a sweet young lady and followed me around, so we started hanging out together. She was a tough little gal, played a lot of sports, and was not afraid to get hit. We used to go down to the creek and shoot bows and arrows. One time, I shot an arrow way up in the sky and wondered where the arrow was. About that time, the arrow fell from the sky and hit her on top of her head. It is crazy as I look back that the arrow didn't hurt her; it just bounced off her head and landed beside her. Unfortunately, her mother came looking for her and made her go home, she didn't like the fact we stayed out late.

Anna had a little brother named George, who was also cool. I treated him like a little brother, probably because of Anna. Their mom made it clear that if I didn't stop hanging out with Anna, she would let me have a piece of her mind. We were just kids, but eventually they moved, and I never saw her again. So much for us and hanging out together, but it sure hurt to lose a friend and such a sweet and beautiful girlfriend.

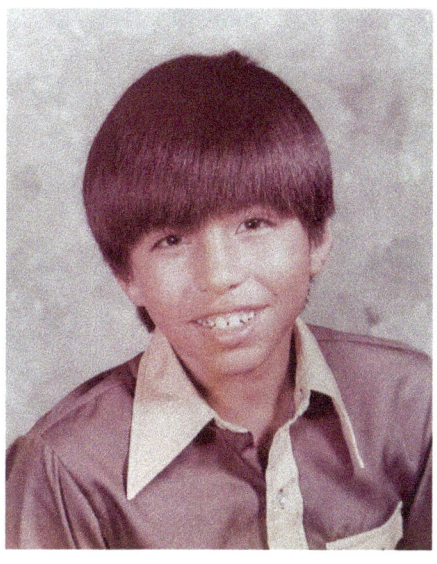

Jorge A. Camacho in the 4th grade

Months passed, and I made new friends. The Fair family moved in next door to us. They were Black and a unique and truly kind family. The most interesting part about them was that they had grown up with Spanish speaking families. Their mother, Guadalupe, was raised in a Spanish speaking environment, and four of their kids had Spanish names: Anita, Marcus, Miguel, and Mario. The father, Mark was the only one with an English name, and he was truly kind. He was a pilot for American Airlines and made lots of money. They were from California and were only looking for a temporary place to live, so they didn't stay long. Mark had a fancy Thunderbird car with suicide doors that was an amazing ride.

The kids were all into sports, and Miguel joined a rock band. He played the bass guitar and was good. Migual also thought he was Bruce Lee in those days. He wore a white sleeveless T-shirt and carried nun-chucks that he swung around all the time. Eventually, he joined a country band and toured the world making a lot of money. We stayed connected for a while, but it became impossible to keep up with him. The family moved to a much bigger and improved home on the other side of Coppell. They were a kind and beautiful family that I greatly admired

I had other friends who lived about two blocks away who came over to our house often. The main reason they liked coming over was to see the two girls across the street. Tammy was a red head with a nice body, and Jodie was just a teenager.

Jodie liked me a lot, and we spent a lot of time together. One day she tested me to see what I would do if we were alone. After her father left for work, she invited me over to watch television. We went to her bedroom to hang out, and when my back was turned, she took off all her clothes except her underwear. She then told me I could touch her breasts. I stood there staring at her, totally shocked and not knowing what to do. I ran off, and she roared with laughter! I never went back to her house. When I told some of my friends, they said I should have taken her up on her offer. Two weeks later they moved away.

David G. Burnett Elementary School

3117 Storey Lane my little brother, Jose "Pepe" Camacho

Meanwhile, at David G. Burnett Elementary School, my cousin Santos and I were still getting into trouble. We both shared an English class, and one day Santos told a joke that made us laugh. We had a bad case of giggles and couldn't stop. Everything everyone said became funny. While we were still laughing the teacher took us out of class into the hallway. We kept on laughing; heck, we even laughed at her. She thought we were on something and asked what the problem was.

We just continued to laugh and giggle at her. Man, I laughed so hard that I let out some gas. She jumped back and screamed, "Who did that?" Needless to say, Santos and I were sent to the principal's office. After we calmed down, we told the principle that we did not know what had gotten into us and apologized for our unruly behavior. We agreed that we would apologize to our English teacher to. He sent us back to class, and we apologized to the teacher and told her it would not happen again. Everything went back to normal, but what a crazy morning that was.

THE FIRST TIME

The day Jodie wanted me to touch her I had simply panicked and didn't know why. I was only about eight or nine years old. I missed an opportunity I thought to myself, but I told myself it would not happen again.

The following year, I was brave and stepped up to the plate.

I used to walk to the 7-Eleven located at Lombardy and Webbs Chapel to get a Slurpee with a superhero on the cup. Over time, I had lots of them. I also would buy bubble gum, which was only one penny. Sometimes I would slip a few pieces of gum in my pocket without paying.

One day, as I was walking home, this young teenage girl driving a cool black Camero stopped and asked if I wanted a ride. Usually, I would turn down the offer because I did not trust strangers. But I thought to myself *this is just a young female, what could she do to me, surely, I could defend myself."* I also thought she might kidnap me, and then other things started running through my head. I looked over and said, "Yes!" I remember being curious why an older female would want to give a ten-year kid a ride.

That's how I met Kelli.

Her Camaro was a sporty 1967 model, and I thought it was a nice car. After that day she would pick me up, and we would roam the area driving past lakes and parks. We also had a lot of fun playing Androids and PACMAN. I thought how cool this is! One day my brother asked me, "Who is this girl, and what are you doing with a girl twice your age?" I told him she didn't bother me and was just a friend. I didn't tell him that I had a hunch she was after me. I figured I would find out soon enough.

Later in life, I always had opportunities with females. I did not have to go far to find them. Like Kelli, they came to me. I must have reminded them of someone they had been with before. I really didn't know why or care why they like me; I just went with the flow.

Back then I had a club house that I built up in a tree. It was the place I went to in order to escape society. I took Kelli there and showed her the place. It had a pole in the center, and I would slide down like Batman and Robin. She thought it was cool, and we had a lot of fun. One day, I told her that I was going to skip school so we could spend the day together. She smiled and said, "Okay." The next day, we met early and guess what: that was the day I really got to know Kelli. Later, I found out this was only her second time to have intercourse.

I did not know anything. I was just ten years old and had no experience with being with a girl. But I was determined to find out and sure wasn't going to let this opportunity get away from me. That day, she was wearing tight blue jeans shorts. She was in a hurry to take them off, and to my surprise, she wasn't wearing any panties. She knew what she was doing and had come prepared ready to have her way with me. She slipped off her white T-Shirt and laid it aside like a blanket. She started touching and playing with my private part, and, man, it started to grow. My eyes rolled back, and I broke out in a cool sweat. She led me, and that first time came and went fast.

Family photo

I will remember her for the rest of my life because we had a beautiful experience, one we shared several more times. She taught me things I never could have imagined and fondling her firm and beautiful breasts was amazing. It seemed we could not get enough of each other.

I thought she was sixteen, but she told me she was going to turn eighteen in a couple of months. I asked her why she wanted to be with someone so young. She simply said, "I always wanted to be with a Spanish person." I guess the day I met Kelli was just my lucky day, she just happened to pick little ole me!

PAINT IN THE CITY

Along with my brother, Beto, and some of his friends, we started hanging out under a bridge sniffing so-called paint. Sniffing became a daily thing and a bad habit for all of us.

We had some bad trips. One day, we were sniffing, and my brother got up and ran away from us. We didn't know what he was doing, and when he returned, he was all scratched up. He told us that he thought we were being attacked. Another time, I was tripping out in the garage at our house on Story Lane. The lights were off in the garage, and I started seeing people with mops for their heads, and they were attacking me. My brother came out and turned the lights on, and they went away. That was crazy; we were crazy.

THE END OF KELLI

Well, my relationship with Kelli didn't end well. Early in my story I shared that I was unbelievably bad and did things that made no sense.

Beto had always been curious why Kelli and I were always hanging around together. One day, he climbed the treehouse and saw me naked with her. After that day, he and his friend Robert would follow us whenever we were together. They were jealous of me.

One Sunday morning, Kelli and I were going to go to the lake, and my brother was determined to go with us, so, he and Robert showed up and we all decided to get high. We started sniffing the paint, and Kelli joined in. Before long, we were all having sex with her; we called it having a shoo…shoo…train her. We thought it was great fun at the time, but that would be the last time I ever saw Kelli. She didn't like the fact we all took advantage of her. I was really sorry, for I liked her so much, and thought she was an amazing person.

ANOTHER SCHOOL - 1976

Around this time, we moved again. This would be my third house and third school. Our address was 3547 Bolivar Drive located between Webb Chapel and Marsh Lane, and I enrolled in Stephen C. Foster Elementary School.

Norberto and Jose Camacho

Our home at 3547 Bolivar Drive

Stephen C. Foster Elementary School

On one of my first days at the school, my six-grade teacher put me in charge of the class one morning. She had to leave to take care of some business and asked me to watch the class. I don't remember why she asked me, but she did. Probably because I was a year older than most of the kids in class. I was older because I didn't start school in Mexico at the same time as other kids. I was not held back, never failed a class, or had to go to summer school. I just started a year later than everyone else.

Alma, Mary, and Pepe having fun in the back yard

While she was gone, a bully named David, whom everyone was afraid of, came up to me and asked if he could borrow my pencil. I said sure and held out the pencil, which he grabbed and threw across the room. He roared with laughter.

I asked, "Why did you do that?" He just kept laughing, so I said, "Please bring my pencil back."

He responded, "Go get it yourself, punk."

The last thing I wanted at this new school was trouble, but he was asking for it, so I stood up, looked at him, and punched him as hard as I could on the chin. Then I punched him again and forcefully said, "Sit down and be quiet." He was shocked and turned red in the face, but he did as I asked.

My wife Belinda DeLa Garza as friends

People in the class started oohing and awing and everything went back to normal. When the teacher returned everyone was doing their assignments, including myself. After class, I overheard classmates asking, "Can you believe what just happened? Jorge whipped David in class!"

Hard to believe now, but sixth grade was when I was introduced to acid, weed, cocaine, and downers. I tried them all to see what they were like. Fortunately, I didn't like the hard stuff because of the side effects. I was more into drinking, smoking weed, and sniffing. I hung around older people just to get high or catch a buzz.

I converted a little room that was connected to the back of our garage into my new club house. This became the place where we would party all the time and sniff to get high. It became my hang-out, where I would escape from society. There, I could get away from the freaky world and live in my fantasy world, which at the time, I thought was all right.

I started getting into fights because of the stuff we were sniffing. We went to the movies after sniffing, and I wouldn't remember anything about the movie. When I sniffed it was a different world for me. One day, I showed up at school with specks of paint on my face and on my shoes and pants. Some of the kids at school knew what I had been doing, but I just ignored them.

Once, my dad came snooping around wondering what we were doing. When he asked us why the room smelled like paint, Beto and I told him that we had been painting the room. Then, we pretended to spray some paint on the walls. We kept getting high on that harmful crap for a long time.

ROCK-N-ROLL

At the time, most of my friends were listening to rock music, so I began to listen to rock as well. I attended my first concert at Moody Coliseum and saw the band Electric Light Orchestra (E.L.O.); the band Sweet who opened for them.

My first concert ticket stub

There was a laser show, and they played their greatest hits, which were spectacular. Sweet was amazing as well, performing their greatest hit at the time, "Love Is Like Oxygen."

I've forgotten a lot about the experience because I was high on weed and drinking beer, but I remember enjoying the music, environment, and the scenery. I also remember trying to impress my older friends by showing them I could handle drugs and alcohol. Unfortunately, I got sick and had to eat a little humble pie.

We lived in the house on Bolivar Drive from 1975 to 1987 or 1988, and during those years I attended all the Texas Jams. I remember hanging out at the RITZ Rock and Roll club in the early 1980's. It was an amazing club, and we had some good times.

Texxas Jam Magazine 1978

Looker, a Rock & Roll Band

I started going to concerts being held in small clubs and in bigger venues like Mother Blues, Arcadia Theater, Tangos, and Reunion Arena. I liked all the old bands: Nazareth, Rush, April-Wine, Jethro Tull, Pink-Floyd, ZZ Top, Trapeze, Robin Trower, Fleetwood Mac, and the Wilsons Sisters just to name a few. I had a vast collection of albums and cassettes. And unbelievably, I had a collection of 8-tracks. Of course, many who are reading this story won't know what an 8-track was.

In 1977, I turned fourteen and was dying to see the band Led Zeppelin. They were scheduled to appear at the Dallas Convention Center on March 4th. I could not wait to purchase a ticket, which was selling for $7.50, $8.50, and $9.50 and going fast. I was lucky to get a ticket for $8.50 because the scalpers were selling them for $15.00, which by today's standards was cheap, but at the time was a lot of money for me.

Led Zeppelin live in concert

Robert Plant was having issues with his voice, so they told everyone they would have to re-schedule. They announced the concert would be held on April 1st of the same year. They picked April Fool's Day! Everyone thought it was a joke, but they were serious.

They played Stairway to Heaven, Rock-N-Roll, Black Dog, Kashmir, Immigrant Song, When the Levee Breaks, Ramble On, Whole Lotta Love, Dazed and Confused, and many more. Jimmy Page's performance on the guitar was impressive, and they had an incredible light show. At one point in the show, they sat on chairs and performed Going to California. The members were John Paul

Jones, Jimmy Page, Robert Plant, and John Bonham (Bonzo). John Bonham's Moby Dick drum solo was amazing, and it was a concert to remember.

Springtime in Dallas, the weather is cool, but not that cold. Therefore, most of the females wore bell bottoms with short tops and blue jean jackets. There were many beautiful young ladies, many with what we called the Wing Hair Style. They parted their hair in the middle, so it looked like they had wings on each side. The style was extremely popular back and genuinely looked good.

I remember my corduroy pants were too short, so I cut each leg off just a little above the ankle and stitched on some fabric from some of my old blue jeans. I had created my own style. At the Zeppelin concert, many people complimented me on the pants and asked where I bought them. I told them, "They are my own creation, and I branded them Macho-Wear."

After the show was over, I was roaming the hallways of the convention center and saw a display stand with many different shirts. One that caught my eye said, "Led Zeppelin North American Tour 1977," I still regret not buying that shirt. I went to many more concerts, but Zeppelin was special. The people, the music, the environment–WOW. I still remember that adventure like it was yesterday.

I'm sure many of you reading my book have had similar experiences. I've listed my email at the end of the book. Please share your thoughts and pictures. I would love to hear from you!

STEPHEN C. FOSTER AND BEYOND

As sixth grade was winding down, I decided to get off the sniffing crap. I knew to keep from getting in more trouble it would be best to not mess with the paint.

I did not get to know many kids at Foster Elementary because they were too straight for me. However, I became friends and hung around with one guy whose Spanish name was Edwardo. The two of us liked the little girls with their cute booties and little breasts. Some did not wear anything underneath their dresses, and we liked touching their private parts. Some of the girls would tell us to stop, and we did, but they really liked being touched. They enjoyed the attention.

Some of my friends and I from the old neighborhood would get young girls high so we could have our way with them. Everyone else was afraid of doing so.

Norberto, Alma, and Mary Camacho

During our time on Bolivar Drive., I attended fifth and sixth grades at Stephen C. Foster Elementary, then moved up to seventh grade at Edward H. Cary Middle School, and ninth grade attended Thomas Jefferson High School, where I graduated from. I was a member of the Class of 1982.

THE ZAPATA'S

The Zapata family lived behind us and was a big family. I kind of stayed away from them even though I kind of liked one of the sisters. I had a crush on her but was afraid that if I showed her, she would tell her brother Arnulfo, who was crazy and wild. I did not want any trouble with him whatsoever.

I had seen him beat up some people badly, and when he didn't think he could handle someone, he would get his friends to help him out. Joe Mama was one of his friends. He was big and heavyset. He was cool, but if you made him mad, he would rough you up. They were members of the United Chicanos gang and wore these amazing jackets. I thought they were cool, but I still stayed away from all of them. None of us wanted any trouble from those guys.

One day after school, this bigger person started to pick on a friend and me. Arnulfo came over and asked if there was a problem. We told him what was going on, and he beat the heck out of the guy. After beating him badly, he looked at him and said, "If I ever run into you again or see anyone else picking on my friends, I will do the same to them. In fact, if I ever hear about anyone even threatening to hurt them, I will come looking for you."

We were like his family, and if anyone was disrespectful to us, they were being disrespectful to him. I remember thinking it was an amazing thing to see. Arnulfo had younger siblings, so I understood where he came from. Or it was just because we lived behind him... who knows? Needless to say, no one ever bothered us again.

CARMEN

Well, so much for the good old times, I used to fight in order to get a little respect. One day after school as I walked home, I saw this person getting beat up by a bigger guy, so I stepped in to help him out. His name was David, and we became best friends for many years. We hung out all the time, and nobody messed with him anymore. We were family, and he was like my brother.

I used to eat over at his house, and his mother, Carmen, became like a mother to me.

Carmen H. Rice *Coffee time for Carmen*

She was great, and I loved and cared for her as if she were my own. If I saw her walking to get groceries. I would drive her. Other times, I picked her up. In fact, if she needed anything, I would do it for her and she knew it. We were all like one big family.

David Rice and me

David had three other older brothers, Tony, Cliff, and Stan, and a little sister named Patty. Tony, David, and I partied and got stoned all the time. We were formidable and liked to roam the neighborhood on our bikes, especially on weekday afternoons and on weekends.

Tony Rice

Tony and Patty Rice

When I entered seventh grade at Cary middle school, I thought the fighting would go away, but it got worse. The so-called older middle schoolers tried to take advantage of me just because I was new. Well, they had another thing coming because I was not going to back down. They learned to respect me.

David Rice, Roxann Kirtley, and Patty Rice

Carmen and Ashley Rice

Patty and Carmen Rice

David and I still hung around together and I was always there if he needed me. We got high after school because it was not easy to get high before school. We did on occasion but decided to put an end to that for a while because the teachers were getting suspicious.

I coasted through seventh grade and made it to the next level. However, I got into more trouble fighting the big dogs at school. On one occasion, I was fighting this guy in the gym and got jumped from behind by two of his friends. But it worked out okay because I knew who they were and told them I would come for them. They couldn't hide from me forever. I eventually got each one, one at a time, and from then on, they were afraid.

Another great concert 1978

That was not a good week. Another day, I was waiting in the gym with everyone else for our coach to tell us what kind of exercises to do. It was a cold and snowy day, which was rare for Dallas. Suddenly this person, I will call John came up from behind me and when I turned, he threw a big snowball in my face. I got up and looked to see who it was. John was friends with the guys I beat up and wanted revenge.

He was known as the biggest and baddest person at the school. I was pissed and upset so I called him out and asked why he had sneaked up from behind me. I called him a coward. He came near and said with a smirky smile, "Are you talking to me."

We started fighting. I hit him with a left and right hook, followed by some upper cuts, but none of my punches fazed him. He was still standing. He came at me with a furious right punch but missed. I knew the only way I would have a chance was to be quick and put some more power in my punches. Then he tried to grab me and pin me down. I gave him a few more punches, and he shook them off. I thought I was doing good because he was getting tired.

I was light on my feet, fast, and moving quickly. Suddenly John landed a punch to the left side of my face, a little to the left of my temple. I started to feel weak and dizzy. I also noticed blood all over the gym floor, and it was not his. Everything stopped and I went straight back where the showers and restrooms were to clean up. The blood was still squirting out. The coach and principal showed up and took me to the nurse who bandaged me up, but the bleeding continued.

Edward H. Cary Middle School class of 1978 - partial picture

The Old Gang: Gilbert, Richard, Tony, and Danny

My parents came to the school, and I was carried out on a stretcher. Everyone looked on as the nurse put me in the back seat. My mother was crying, which bothered me, for I didn't like seeing her like that. Fortunately, I turned out that I wasn't hurt too badly. John had been wearing a ring which did most of the damage.

I accepted defeat and chalked it up to a loss. I won some, I lost some, but I got better just like practicing for football. Practice, practice, and more practice, which I did afterward for many days. Every evening, I hit the punching bag and the speed bag which were in our garage. I had always wanted to be a boxer.

I was taught that every fight would be different and that I would need to stay focused no matter what. That last fight had caught me off guard because I tried to attack with my speed instead of fighting smart. We aren't supposed to dwell on past mistakes but move on and learn from them.

After about two weeks, I was completely healed and a little more prepared. The coach had given us an excellent work out that day, and I was waiting in line to get some water at the back of the gym near the restrooms. I noticed this tall Black guy I'll call Joe, which was not his real name. He was waving for students to get out of his way. He got upset with me and tried to splach water on me from the fountain. I said, "No you don't."

He replied, "what are you going to do about it?"

I thought *boy here we go again*. I did my absolute best to avoid fighting him, but I was not going to let anyone push me around. At the time, I thought others needed to see me stand up to him so that they didn't have to be scared when bullied or pushed around. I decided to fight him for all those watching who didn't know how to defend themselves. Educating them became my motivation.

Tony Valdez and Me

THE UPS AND DOWNS OF J.C.

James Rodgers and me

However, the last thing I wanted was to go home bleeding and see my mother in tears. Not happening this time, NO...NO...NO! I acted like I was taking off my shirt, so he started to do the same. But I had planned to set the tone for the fight, so while he was unbuttoning his shirt, I acted like I was going to punch him and he jumped back. It was an old trick just to catch your opponent off guard. Then, I quickly pulled off my white T-shirt, which was the style back in the day.

Immediately, I caught him with a couple left hooks, then a right hook, and some furious upper cuts. I had been working on putting my weight behind my punches, and they were doing him damage. He could not run because a ring of students had formed around us. He had no choice but to fight his way out. I hit him many times, but you really couldn't tell how bad it was because he had a dark, black complexion. Not that I have anything against black or anything like that, for I have a lot of Black friends. I noticed tears coming out of his eyes and running down his face. I figured the fight was over, so I stopped and started walking away. That's when he picked up a wooden bench and came towards me.

Edward H. Cary Middle School

I had to think fast, so I pushed the bench away, shoved him to the gym floor, and started hitting him. Soon he was just lying there in pain. He indicated he did not want any more trouble. I put my shirt back on and those around us let me by. On one end of the gym some people yelled, "Great round, Camacho, way to go! You defeated the bully." I felt good inside because I had just defeated one of the top dogs in our school. I had finally gotten respect, and no one ever messed with my friends or me again.

Tony Hunter, some Classmates, and me

Edward H. Cary Middle School class of 1978 - partial picture

Joe had a lot of friends, but later that day I was on the bus going home, and I saw him walking alone with his head down and looking sad. I felt bad for him because I was a good person. I wasn't the one who had been looking for trouble. I just did what needed to be done at the time.

My eighth grade class, first period

Draft class, third Period

My two friends, Esther & Becky

The next day as I was eating lunch in the cafeteria when John who had hit me with his ring started making fun of Joe, whom I had beaten the day before. He was ribbing him for getting beat and could not believe it was me that defeated him. He started distancing himself from him. In the back of my mind I was thinking, on any given day I could do the same to John that I had to Joe.

THE GOOD TIMES IN HIGH SCHOOL

When I entered ninth grade at Thomas Jefferson, everyone knew me. My older brother was attending at the time, but later decided to drop out. I continued my normal routine of getting high after school and occasionally before. Drugs were part of our daily lives, and we all knew the people who sold the drugs. The weed was ten dollars a bag, which was a lot. For that reason, most kids were growing their own, and I grew mine as well.

I mixed my weed plants in with my dad's tomato plants in our back garden. My dad would look at the plants, scratch his head, and comment about how interesting and wild they looked. Wild, but beautiful!

In those days, there was no such thing as crack cocaine. We were all about weed, downers, and acid. Many of us went to concerts and had an enjoyable time. Those were good times. Mondays were a special day at the movies. The big Gemini drive-in on Forest Lane was another hang out. At the time, if you were living in Dallas, you knew where the theater was because everyone used to hang out there to party and have fun. Or to pick up some babes.

Another place we went to was Emerald or Manana racing strips. It was fun to see those cars and bikes race. We hung around on the side of the road, drank a few beers, smoked some reefers, and got stoned. All the racing action was impressive, and we just soaked it in.

We also went to the Bluffs and Brownwood Park. One summer, I met this incredibly young and pretty girl named Marie. I loved her so much. We went everywhere together. We went to concerts, movies, and made love everywhere we went. However, I did not get to stay with her long because she was just in town visiting family for that summer. Her parents were getting a divorce. Anyway, the time I was with her was incredible.

Nazareth at the TEXXAS Jam 1979

Nazareth live in concert

That summer, I had an amazing time.

MY FIRST JOB

Safeway Food Store was only a couple of blocks from where I lived, so I applied for a job, and they hired me for a part-time position. I started the tenth grade right after getting the job. Many things were happening at the time, and I was not sure how everything was going to turn out.

There was school, there was work, and there were family problems. My parents were having issues, and I was incredibly determined to keep the family together in any way possible. I helped pay the mortgage bill and anything else that was needed. I thought about dropping out of school and joining the Army, but deep inside, I could hear my father's voice telling me that education was especially important. I also got encouragement from one of my teachers to stay and get my high school diploma. So, I partied, worked, and continued going to school. I did my best to forget things at home. Life was overwhelming at times.

Safeway Food Stores, Inc.

Thomas Jefferson High School

THE UPS AND DOWNS OF J.C.

Ticket stubs

Judas Priest in the early 1980s

LIVING THE DREAM

For the next few months, I was working as a package clerk. My store manager, Mr. Wesson, was a unique person who approached me one day when it was pouring outside and said he wanted to speak to me. I asked him to please hold on for a moment while I helped this elderly person get her groceries to her car.

TEXXAS WORLD MUSIC FESTIVAL 1979

TEXXAS JAM poster 1979

On the way back inside, I grabbed several shopping carts and returned them to the store. I always believed in helping customers, knowing if you took care of them, they would come back. Then they would tell someone about their experience and that person would tell someone else and that person would tell someone, and before you knew, more customers would be shopping at our store. Good customer service is necessary. People want to shop where they are welcome, and employees treat them like they want to be treated. SAFEWAY FOOD STORE #161, was like that.

MR. WESSON believed in customer service. He stood there patiently and was getting wet, but he didn't seem to mind. We had a long, pleasant conversation, and he ended up offering me a promotion. He wanted to know if I would go to the produce department, and it didn't take long for me to decide. I was excited about becoming a Produce Clerk. No one seemed to like working there because it was an extremely hard job. People who worked in the department didn't stay long because it was too much of a challenge.

ZZ TOP's Billy Gibbons on New Year's Eve in 1980

ZZ TOP ticket stub

I had so much fun working in the produce department. I got lost in work, and the weeks seemed to fly by.

THE JOURNEY CONTINUES

Things were going well at work and school, but things at home remained the same. Many days, I would work late because I did not want to go home to deal with the situations there. Looking back, I don't know how I did it.

My first car 1970 Malibu Chevelle

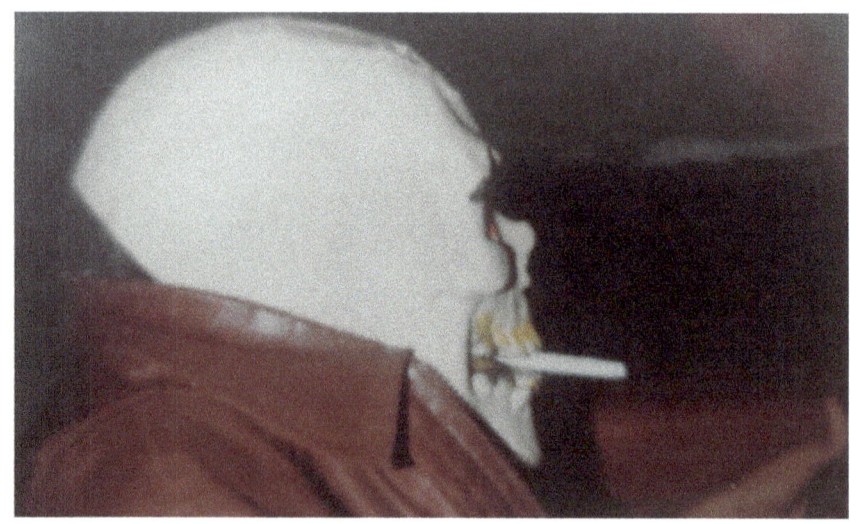

I'm heading to the Jethro Tull concert on Halloween night

At the concert

At times, I thought about leaving like my older brother and older sister, but they always returned when they could not make their relationships work out. One time, my older sister returned pregnant. I tell you her situation sure caused some problems around the house. My folks were not getting along, and my father blamed the pregnancy on my mother.

Anyway, leaving home was not the right answer; besides, I was still a minor. I knew my family needed me, and I couldn't walk out on my mother. Coming from a family that worked hard and did not have time for school, she was not well educated.

She was old school and had a decent job, but did not know how to manage her money. I did most of that for her. I would make out a budget and put money aside to pay the bills, buy food, and make the mortgage payment every month. Even though I was not that good at math, I could add, subtract, multiply, and divide. I was also trying to keep my little brother and my two little sisters together. They were my main priority because we were family.

My little brother tried to help and contributed cash to the family by doing yard work and other odd jobs. I was always looking for better ways to get more money the right way, the legal way. I was now in 11th grade, and I knew like it was going to be extremely hard to finish, but I continued to study hard and managed to pass most of my tests. The subject that gave me the most trouble was math with all the symbols. Everyone else I knew aced math, but not me. It just made me study and read more, which I did not mind. That year seemed to go fast because I was working a lot after school. My increased focus on schoolwork was paying off.

In the winter of 1981, I made a snowman in front of our house. It had been snowing a lot, and school closed for a few days, so I decided to enjoy the time off. I took a few pictures of my two beautiful little sisters, Alma, and Mary. We also added a new baby to the family, my nephew whom I treated like a little brother. My older sister was not able to raise her baby, so Mother had him live with us, and from that time on she raised him.

My nephew Nuno Camacho

UNBELIEVABLE TIMES

I was making good money and living life. I continued to party, go to concerts, and was dating different girls. I don't know how, but I managed to keep my job. Sometimes, I woke up with an unbelievably bad headache (hang-over and was tired and weak. I thought everyone acted that way, and my actions were all part of growing up. To tell the truth, that's when my alcohol addiction began.

THE UPS AND DOWNS OF J.C.

My second festival 1979

I thought to have a fun time a person needed to drink and get high. I also thought it was okay to take advantage of girls and just use them. They didn't seem to mind. Looking back, we were just using each other. I did not want to be tied down to any one girl because I knew I could have many of the girls I encountered. There were some nice ones, but there were some crazy ones too. The way I treated those girls did not make any sense; it was all about the sex for me. Now I know that I was wrong to treat them the way I did.

Genesis in concert in the early 1980s

Some of my friends went to the Harry Hines area and messed around with hookers. They just wanted to be able to tell guys at school that they had been with an older woman. They were just showing off and being crazy.

At the beginning of my senior year, I was called to the principal's office to talk about my future. They told me that if I kept doing well, I could miss the second half of my senior year and still graduate with my classmates. I was on track to be able to build up enough credits by doing well on my tests.

Phil Collins in concert

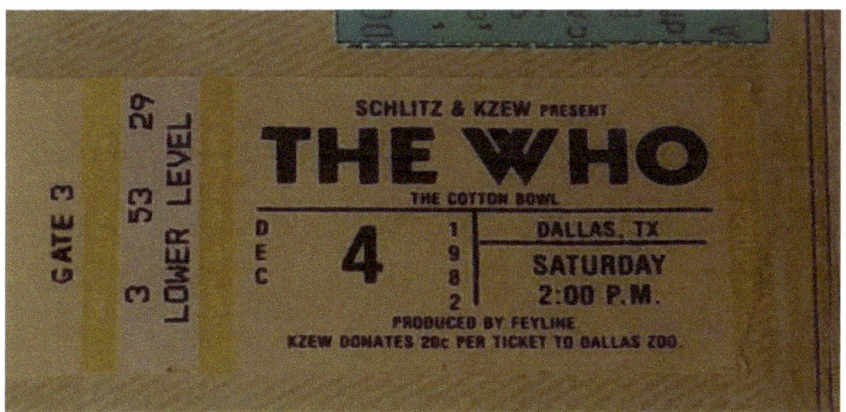

The WHO live in concert

However, I found myself drinking increasingly more, so I decided to party only on weekends. I was more determined to get my homework done, so I studied harder than ever before. I was not going to let all my hard work go down the drain.

The WHO's PeteTownshend

THE UPS AND DOWNS OF J.C.

Seniors 1982

Father, Jesus O. Camacho

In the produce department I did not feel that I was performing like I should, so I talked to my manager about being a stocker. The partying and drinking made me a different person. I tried to make changes in life and thought working shifts with the night crew would help. Instead, I started drinking and partying with them every day. My behavior was getting worse, so I decided to get off the night crew, but I continued to get high and drink.

My high school diploma

I was confused about what I wanted out of life. Something was missing. After graduation, I didn't have school to worry about, and the way I was living did not provide any answers. As my life journey continued, I started working shifts as a cashier during the day, which was awkward. However, the move provided an opportunity for me to also stock the dairy department, which included beer and wine. I liked that I had the flexibility to leave the check-out stand, goof around, and help out the other checkers sack groceries.

I could work in any department in the store. I was knowledgeable about every position: dairy, beer & wine, office, meat department, and of course the produce department. Which I had abandoned for a while.

Thomas Jefferson High School class of 1982

Thomas Jefferson High School Mascot

The area looked different than when I had worked there before, and it was beckoning me to return. Two months later, I accepted the invitation to return as the third shift. I wondered what the heck was going on because the department looked nice and pretty during the day, but the evening hours were a different story. I wanted to make sure the customers shopping at night enjoyed the same treatment as customers during the day. They too deserved a nice and well-stocked department. Everyone was open to my ideas, so I made having the department looking good in the evening seven days a week a priority.

The management was curious to see what was being sold in the evening. At times, they noticed we were running out of key items and losing sales as a result. That's where I came in and provided help. Most weekdays I would help set up in the morning and then maintain the department in the evening. I focused on key sale items to keep well stocked.

I also made sure the floor was free from slippage. Grapes and other items could fall on the floor and cause a person to slip and fall. In those days, some customers looked for a way to file a lawsuit. That was unacceptable to me, and I planned to keep them from being able to do so. We put extra precautions in place and posted flyers on the back bulletin board to create more employee awareness.

BAD CHOICES

The more I worked the more I convinced myself it was okay to drink and party. Well, everything went fairly good for a couple of years, but in 1983 I had trouble with the law.

I was at the Beggers Club with a friend, playing pool, and we were beating everyone. The other players started to get upset, and by the look on their faces, they didn't seem to like that we were Spanish. Anyway, the smoke and body heat in the place started to get to me so I decided to go outside and get some fresh air. When I tried to return one of the door bouncers named Richard would not let me back inside.

I began arguing with him, but he still refused to let me in. I told him that I had paid and showed him the entry stamp on my hand. He said he did not care. He started pushing and shoving me back.

Before I knew what was happening, I was surrounded by Richard's friends, some of whom were the people we had been beating at pool. Well, my so-called friend came to look for me, saw what was happening, and ran off. I call him a so-called friend because a real friend would stick around and help no matter what, even if they risked a beating as well.

I did not know what to do, so I pulled out a small looking knife that I used in the produce department to scare them, but with no luck. One of them came up on one side of me while two of the others knocked me off my feet. I was still holding the knife and when one tried to take the knife away, I moved quickly and cut his hand. There were too many of them to handle so I decided not to defend myself. I got up and ran as fast as I could, not knowing where I was going.

I almost got run over by the moving cars because it was dark outside. I remember seeing headlights as I ran across the street to get away from them. They were yelling at me to stop. I thought I had outrun them, but then I slipped on some gravel crossing at a parking lot. As I was getting up, someone tackled me from behind. Soon, I heard footsteps approaching and the rest of the guys arrived and started beating me. They kicked me in the face, ribs, jaw, and my head. My body was aching, and I had a terrible headache, which was the result of the beating, but it could have very well been due to all the drinking. All I knew was I felt dizzy.

When the police got there, they told them that I had gone crazy and tried to cut them all. They arrested me and took me into custody. They didn't believe what I said because there were more of them, and I did not have a witness. I was taken to the city jail on Main Street in downtown Dallas. My family eventually got me out.

My so-called friend told them I got into trouble because of all the drinking. They called an attorney who informed us that one of the guys had been stabbed in the side and had been taken to the hospital bleeding. I did not realize that a small knife could do so much damage.

I panicked, wondering what kind of damage I had done. I did not know what to do so I promised myself that I would never drink again. I asked God to please help me, and if He let the person live, I would quit drinking and become better organized. I would continue working to make lots of money and act like nothing ever happened. But, deep inside of me, I had this fear and was troubled by it. The attorney told us the man would survive.

The lawyer did a terrible job because he just wanted to close the case. Instead of fighting for me, he pushed for 10 years of deferred probation, which was not fair at all. Later, I told him so, and he said that was the best he could do. He just wanted our money.

I tried to get my life back on the right track. I went to Alcohol Anonymous (AA) meetings and worked like there would be no tomorrow. I did my best to avoid trouble. Because of the issues my parents were having, which I did not fully understand, I knew I needed to be there for my younger brother and two wonderful little sisters.

OLD WAYS

Two years passed and life seemed good, I even bought a new 1985 Monte Carlo. I wanted the SS, but Chevrolet was having issues with the model that year. I was working my ass off, but little by little the old lifestyle started calling. I started to miss the wildlife, the good times, and the women.

Our house at 3137 Waldrop Street

My wonderful family

Tom Thumb pride

I went to see Ozzy Osborne and Black Sabbath with some friends, and we all piled into my new Monte Carlo. On the way home, I ran a red light and then a stop sign. My friends were just waiting for the impact. I was fortunate we didn't get hit or cause an accident. They encouraged me to slow down and be more careful.

I ignored them and was pulled over by two police officers. They were rude and were giving us all a tough time. They found some weed in the car and charged me for reckless driving. They threw me in the back seat of their police car and told me not to come out.

I really needed to use the restroom badly, so I managed to open the door and asked permission. They told me to stay in the car. I begged them both to at least let me go by a large dumpster that was nearby.

The lady officer said, "No!"

So, I said, "Here it goes."

I peed in my pants. My friends looked at me and felt sorry for me.

INCARCERATION

Anyway, my stupidity got me 180-days of shock probation. Ann Richards had a revolving door policy and shock probation allowed a judge to send a previously convicted offender to a short term in jail in hopes of rehabilitation. They sent me to the state prison in Navasota, Texas.

After serving my time, I went back in front of a judge in Dallas County. I pleaded with the judge to have mercy on me and that I would do everything to change my lifestyle. I told him that prison was not for me. He reinstated my previous probation but told me that if I got in trouble of any kind, he would throw the book at me.

My Mother, Tia Lupe, Tio Tele, and sister Mary

I returned to work, went to AA meetings, and avoided people I thought were trouble, but before long, I started drinking and partying all over again. Soon, I found myself in the Salvation Army, which was a place where you could go and sober up and then leave.

Welcome home party

THE UPS AND DOWNS OF J.C.

Tio Juan, Tio Ramiro, and Me

They had lots of people that were there because of their drinking. There were many homeless people, and you could tell who the homeless were because their clothes had been worn for days, even weeks. I often gave those people money because I knew they really needed help. It was the way I was brought up. My mother taught me compassion; it ran in our family. She would talk to and provide help to anyone whether she knew them or not.

JORGE A. CAMACHO

Mother, Uncle Poncho, and Tia Lupe

My Father

During this time, I asked myself many times why all this was happening to me. I started to think I had a drinking problem. Then I would convince myself I didn't. I kept denying there was a problem.

Before long I was sent back to prison for a two-year sentence. I was incredibly lucky that I only received two years. T.D.C. was having an overcrowding crisis those days, and the state did not have a solution. I was able to dodge another bullet because I ended up doing only six and half months. Someone upstairs was watching over me and was trying to get my attention.

I said goodbye to my homeboys in Huntsville and was on my way. I took a taxi to the nearest airport so I could catch a Southwest flight home. Before I left, I had told my family when I got out, I was never going to drink again. But on the flight home I started drinking beer. Sure, was nice having my freedom back, but I knew something was missing.

Mother and sister Alma

Mother, Beto and his wife Tonya

At home, we had a celebration and called it "getting out of the military party" to make it sound joyful. We invited a few close friends, my uncles, and some other family members. Of course, I continued drinking and was a total mess.

Soon after being released from THE WALLS in Huntsville, Texas I repeated my old patterns: drinking, smoking weed, and spending time with hookers. I could not believe what I was doing, but still would not admit to having a problem. I was in total denial.

Produce Department at Tom Thumb

Wet-rack at Tom Thumb

As required, I reported to my parole officer and submitted a monthly report. I did so well that the officer told me I only had to report every other month. He instructed me to work, stay busy, and not get into trouble with the law, or he would have to do what was necessary.

I continued my old ways drinking like a fish and getting high, however, I avoided trouble and stayed off the street. I was free once again, but I felt this void inside that did not make any sense.

I started dating various ladies some my age and some older looking to fill the hole in my heart. I was not happy and found myself arguing with them about any little thing. Some tried to control me, and I did not want to be tied down.

My first promotion at Tom Thumb 1989

Me at Tom Thumb 1989

TOXIC FEMALES

ROBIN

Then I met Robin, a young girl from Oklahoma. She was small and stood five and half feet tall. She had beautiful hazel eyes and was extremely outgoing, plain nice all around. Man, did it take me forever to get into her pants. She loved to test me by playing female head games to see if I really liked her. But I tell you, having sex with her was sure worth the wait.

Another hang out

We spent lots of time together hanging out and enjoying each other's company. She would call me at work or at home and say, "Let's get fogged," which was just an expression meaning let's hang out and drink some beer, wine, and liquor. I jumped at the opportunity every time.

She had this so-called roommate named Scott who was an old friend. Turns out he was gay and not into females. He had his own room, so at first it did not bother me that he lived with her. Besides, he stayed in his room most of the time and as long as I was getting satisfied, everything was okay.

Back to work

However, once I started to fall in love with her, my attitude began to change. I got a little jealous of Scott, for I did not want another male anywhere near her. I was thinking about marrying her. I started working a second part-time job to keep me busy and to help me stay out of trouble. I wanted to settle down and escape the bad, crazy life I had been living. To me, Robin seemed perfect, we could relate to things, and she made me happy. I could trust her, or so I thought!

One day she called me at work and asked what time I was coming over. I told her it would be around 4 o'clock. Business was slow that day at the store and we finished stocking the shelves by 1:30. My boss asked me if I wanted to leave early, saying it was up to me. I had worked a lot of hours. It had been a long week, and I had not even had time to deposit my check.

I thought about Robin and wanted to be with her, so I took my manager up on his offer and headed over to see her. She and I were together all the time, sometimes at her apartment and sometimes at my house. I had been thinking about asking her to move in with me, I was already helping out with paying the rent, bills, and food. But I had hesitated because I did not know her that well.

Robin and me getting ready for Halloween

When I got to her apartment that day, I noticed her car, so I sat for a while in my candy apple red 1966 Buick Skylark convertible, my pride and joy at the time. The car had a three hundred cubic inch V-8 engine with an original 2-barrel carburetor and an automatic Super Turbine 2-speed transmission. I finished my beer while daydreaming about getting married and what our life together would be like.

My produce department at store #27

Suddenly some movement caught my attention, and I noticed a male coming out of her apartment. He was about my size with a slim build, clean shaven, and had short brown hair. I knew it was not her roommate because Scott was at work and didn't get home until five or six depending on his schedule. I wondered who in the world could this person be leaving so fast.

I got out of my car and headed upstairs. Robin was drunk and looked like she had just stepped out of the shower. Her hair was partially wet, and she was wearing a long, green T-shirt with nothing else on but her underwear. She asked, "Hey babe. What are you doing home so early?"

I turned around and walked back to my car. I figured I could get my belongings later. I spun out and drove away. She called me and tried to explain. She said, "We just had some drinks but did not do anything physical," which I refused to believe. Seeing what she was wearing was enough for me and I did not want to have anything else to do with her.

Later she tried to get me back by apologizing and saying we could work things out. Then, she said she would take me back on one condition, I had to stop drinking. I told her, "Heck no, you are the one with the problem!" I thought it best to forget her.

I started partying to drain away my sorrows. After work I would start drinking. I would remember getting drunk but not knowing how I got home. It seemed that every time I got into trouble drinking was involved. But I continued to deny I had a problem.

Tom Thumb Food and Pharmacy

My 1966 SkyLark convertible

One night, I parked my Buick convertible on the street and was walking. The cops picked me up and took me to jail for public intoxication. When I was released ten hours later, I went looking for my car but couldn't find it anywhere. I thought it had been stolen. A friend of mine told me to wait until the next day and I would probably remember where I left the car.

OLD RED

I started hanging out with this girl named Old Red (Red) who I had known since she was about sixteen years old. She had been okay looking back then, but now she had and blossomed and looked much nicer.

THE UPS AND DOWNS OF J.C.

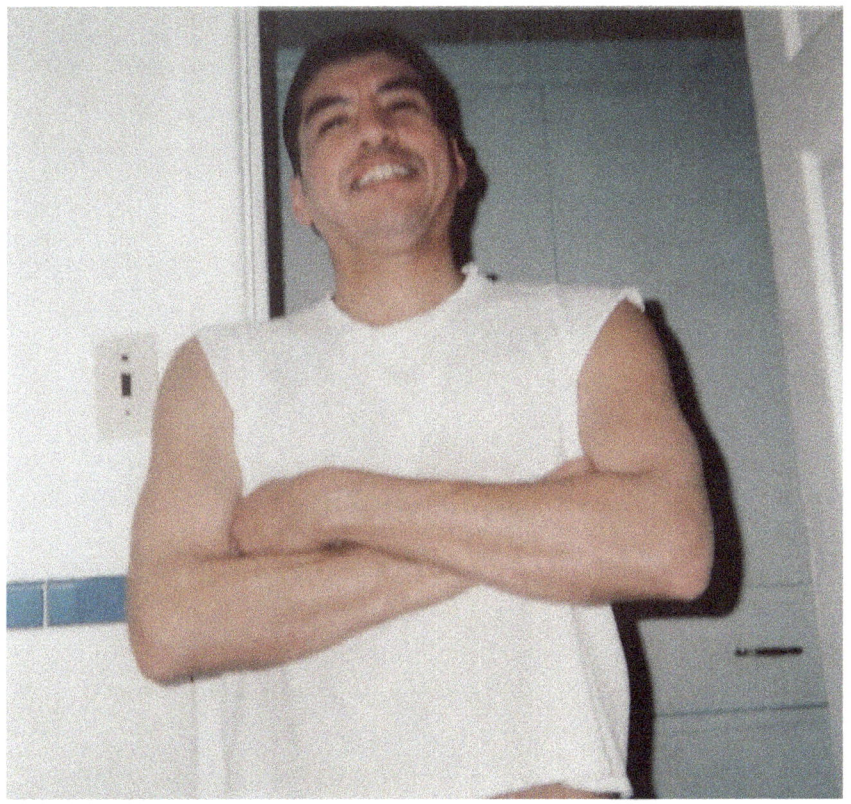

A day off from Tom Thumb

She was dating one of my best friends whom I had grown up with but kept coming over to my place to see me. Part of the reason she wanted to hang out with me was to get back at him. She would tell me about their problems, but that she loved him. Which I thought was odd since she was spending time with me. I knew she wanted something; I could feel it.

Old Red relaxing

Partying at the park with Red

THE UPS AND DOWNS OF J.C.

Old Red and her Mother, Jo Berry

I justified being with her thinking that if she wanted to give me a piece of her pie, she must like me as well. The first time we were together, she got me drunk, and I was brave enough to take advantage of the situation. Later, I learned she had a drug problem and would do anything to get her dope.

She told me, "When you are drinking, you do crazy things and get mighty brave." My drinking did not improve; it got worse. I found myself drinking more around her and doing dope. There were days that I did not sleep well, or I would go without sleeping.

Well, we hung around together and ended up dating and became boyfriend-girlfriend. It was on Mother's Day in 1994 that I made her mine by giving her a silver chain. She had a daughter named Ashley whom I adored.

DRINKING AND DRIVING

It was around this time that I was introduced to crack cocaine. For me, it was a cleaner high, but much more addictive. There were many people who could not get off that drug.

One night, I was drinking and doing dope in Coppell, a suburb of Dallas. It was getting late so I decided to take the freeway home because it would be faster. I was driving my Skylark, and a Farmers Branch Police officer pulled me over and charged me with a D.W.I.

Behind bars

My little brother bailed me out the next day. Still, I continued to deny I had a problem. However, I did feel a deep void. I really did not even know what had happened. I was working for Tom Thumb at the time, which was owned by the Cullum Company, an excellent company to work for. Fortunately, I was off that day. As soon as I was released, I continued to party all over again. Everyone but me thought I was crazy and insane.

Super-Bowl ready at store #27

Promotional display at store #27

Holiday ready at store #27

I used the drugs and alcohol to forget about life problems. In my twisted mind, I thought I was hanging with a good crowd. I thought doing dope and partying was just a normal part of life. On Saturday of that same week I was with the same people in Coppell and around 10:30 P.M., I finally decided to call it night and head home. Wanting to stay clear of the freeway, I took a different route on Luna Road. I just wanted to go home and get some much-needed rest. Suddenly, a car heading in my direction looked like it was going to hit me. I swerved to miss the car, ran off the road, and ended up in a small ditch full of water. My car died. I tried and tried to re-start it, but to no avail. I thought to myself, "*I just want to go home.*" I had this feeling of Déjà vu "*why is this happening and why me?*"

Arrested for D.W.I.

Tom Thumb Page and Pharmacy at Cullum Company

When the car wouldn't start, I became increasingly frustrated. I opened the hood to check the carburetor to see if there was something I could do to fix it. The car was flooded so I waited quite a while in hopes that it would start. I was tired and wanted to avoid a long walk home. I finally gave up and started to walk when a big dump truck stopped next to my car and then took off. I thought it was weird that the driver didn't ask if I needed help.

Before long, I noticed a police car with lights flashing coming up behind me. The officer asked me if it was my car by the side of the road. I excitedly told him, "Yes, it is my car, a crazed driver almost hit me, and I veered off to avoid an accident and now it won't start." I figured the dump truck driver might have called the police and reported an accident or thought it was a stolen car.

"Have you been drinking? Do you think you can pass our sobriety test?" The police officer asked.

I responded as confidently as I could, "Yes, I can pass." But then I changed my answer saying, "Well I had a few beers, so I probably won't pass."

Heck, the one thing I did know was that I wasn't sober. It didn't take a genius to see that I was tired and had way too much alcohol in my system. He obviously knew it as well and along with his partner they smiled and asked if I could walk thirty steps backwards. They were having some fun at my expense.

I told them, "On my best day I couldn't walk backwards like that, so I guess you might as well arrest me." Which they did, and I got a ride to the Carrollton Police Department. I remember thinking, "*Why didn't they just help me?*" Instead, they charged me with D.W.I. which was my second in two weeks. My car ended up in the same place as before, the auto pound.

Because they didn't help me, I gave all the officers a tough time. First, I wet some toilet tissue and covered up the camera afraid they were watching me. Then I stopped up the toilet and sink and the water went everywhere. I started banging my head on the iron bars until I bled so I could say that one of the officers had beaten me with a club. I was taken to a nearby hospital where they treated me and promptly returned me to jail.

A few days passed, and then they transferred me to the Farmers Branch Police Department. The reason I was told was because of my outstanding tickets. Once again, my little brother was ready to pay the $1,300 required for my bail. However, he was told he would need to go to Dallas County to make bail. They would release me upon finalization of the formal paperwork in a day or two. It is great to have family members who care, and he was one I could always count on.

The day came, and I was released around midnight. My brother asked, "Why aren't you wearing any shoes?" I looked down and wondered what the heck happened to my shoes. It didn't make any sense to me. We asked the releasing officer, and he told us that I didn't have shoes when I was brought in and booked. I just figured someone liked my shoes and took them, I didn't know.

Barefooted, I headed toward home with my brother. Since I had my wallet, I asked him to stop at an Exxon gas station so I could buy him some gas. I was already craving a cold beer so when I went inside to pay, I bought a twelve pack of Budweiser. I told myself it was okay if I had just one beer. Unfortunately, that was the reasoning that led to all of my binges. I would have one beer and then convince myself it was okay to have another, and before long I couldn't stop drinking and ended up drunk. I had a problem: I was an alcoholic and had no clue.

After a few weeks, my court date finally arrived for my first D.W.I. and I had a good attorney. The female judge laughed as she read what was in the police report, "The arresting officer asked the suspect his name and asked to see his driver's license. The suspect showed him a dollar bill and told the officer that was his picture on the bill." I could not remember anything I said. Fortunately, my attorney was able to get me off, because the arresting officer was alone. It was his word against mine, and he had no witnesses.

The second D.W.I. was a different story. Pretty hard to beat considering I told the police I had been driving when a reckless driver tried to run me off the road. Given the other driver's behavior my attorney was able to get me five years' probation.

I knew I needed to make a change; my life was out of control. I wanted to settle down and have a normal life. Instead, I continued to party and have fun. I was just living in a fantasy world.

SERGIO'S PLACE AND KAREN

Sergio's place was located near Harry Hines in Dallas, Texas. The area was full of a variety of shops and warehouses from leather shops to body shops to machine shops. Sergio's house was unique and hidden among a few other homes in the area. It was the second house from the corner and had lots of parking spaces. I used to park up front where I could keep an eye on my white and cream-colored 1964 Impala, which was another one of my pride and joys.

The car was 95% original with a 327-cu. ft. engine, a four-barrel carburetor, chrome trimmings, bucket seats, and a four on the floor gear shift. The other 5% was due to my addition to a great sound system complete with two four-way, Pioneer speakers in the back windows on each side, three-way speakers mounted on the passenger door and the driver's door, and an amazing speaker in the middle of the back seat. The rally wheels I added gave the vehicle a cool, sporty look that attracted lots of people. Unfortunately, thieves were among those who admired my ride...

Karen and me at her Apartment

What a ride it was! I met lots of people at Sergio's. People were always coming and going, so I saw different people every time I went, especially on weekends. Everyone would party and get high. That's where I met Karen, a true southern woman who was beautiful with a light tan and green eyes. It was known that she was a rebel from the south.

One Friday after partying, I decided to leave early because I had to get up early for work the next day. Karen followed me outside and asked me to stay a while longer. I declined and told her I would see her the next time I came to Sergio's. For the next two weeks, I kept a low profile and focused on my work.

Sergio did not go out much and was always home on weekends. I returned one Friday night, and he and some friends were watching television. They were really into western movies and wrestling. Sergio told me that Karen had been asking about me and wanted to know if I was married or had a girlfriend. She also wanted to know where I lived. He told me she was very interested in me. *What a crazy woman.* I thought to myself. *Aren't they all, with just different names?* So, I decided it was best not to hang around and went cruising. I went to the carwash and took my time washing and grooming my pride and joy. Then, I went over to the River Chon Park area where my friends like to hang out and play music. They were playing their guitars and had drummers and singers. They rocked the area with their sound.

Heavy Metal the movie track

I decided to hang out at Sergio's the next day and arrived around 1:00 p.m., Karen was there. Everyone was watching the movie "Heavy Metal" which I had seen when it first came out. I thought it was a cool and interesting movie. I sat on one side of the couch where no one else was sitting and Karen looked over, smiled, and asked, "Would you like a cold beer?"

I said, "Sure." She left the room, and when she returned, she handed me a Longneck Budweiser, which just happened to be my favorite brand. I assumed Sergio told her I was a Bud-Man, but I never knew for sure if he did.

Next thing I know, she plops down onto the couch next to me and asked, "Where have you been."

"I've been extremely busy." I responded as if I were not interested. However, she had this unique personality to which I was drawn.

I could tell by her eyes that she didn't believe me. She thought I had a girlfriend who kept me on a tight leash.

Sergio was running low on beer, so I volunteered to go to the store. I went out the door, and the next thing I knew, Karen was climbing into on the passenger side of my car. In her eyes, I saw trouble but decided to go with the flow. We ended up at a Centennial Liquor store, and she went inside with me. When I asked her if she wanted anything, she grabbed a six pack of Zima, which was a wine cooler in a clear looking bottle with a high volume of alcohol.

1965 Buick Oldsmobile Cutlass

On our return trip, she told me that I was a cool person, and she was into me. I thought to myself, *I like being single and don't want you or anyone else holding me back*. However, deep down I wanted to know more about her, so we hung out for a while. It started getting late, and darkness had settled in outside, so I decided to head home. Karen asked if I would give her a ride, and I said, "Sure."

She began telling me about herself and wanting to gain my trust she told me she worked in a strip club and had a drug problem. She also said she had a craving and asked me to take her to find some drugs.

I took her to some neighborhood over by Love field. People were coming up to us asking how much dope we wanted. She waved them off, saying she was looking for Shorty. Not seeing him anywhere she told me where he lived, and I drove to a complex near Bachman Lake. She said all the people who were talking to us sold fake drugs. Once we arrived at Shorty's, she asked me to wait and to please be patient. I said, "Okay," as she was exiting the car.

After a few minutes, a heavy-set man approached me and asked if I would give him a ride. I said, "I am waiting for someone and can't leave." He got a little upset, and I started feeling like something bad was about to happen. He was standing to my left, and my heart started to race. I didn't want to show that I was nervous or show any weakness, so I just ignored him waiting for Karen.

Suddenly, I had this dreamlike vision. He was climbing in the back seat of my car directly behind me after I agreed to take him where he wanted to go. He pulled out a gun and shot me in the back of the head, and I fell to one side. Karen walked up, and when she saw what happened, she ran off screaming.

I snapped out of the dream when Karen returned and got into the car. As we drove off the guy was just standing there with his hands in his jacket pockets. I was freaked out. She asked me what the person wanted. I told her that I thought he wanted to sell me some dope and that he told me you were just a trick and no good.

She smiled at me and gave me that crazy look. I could not believe that Karen had a drug problem; she was just too healthy and good-looking. When I dropped her off at her friend's house, she asked me If I wanted to come inside. I said no thanks, that I needed to get some rest. She kissed me on my cheek and then flashed her breasts at me. Somewhat taken back I laughed and asked, "Are those real."

Driving away the thought occurred, *I came close to dying tonight, but something kept it from happening.* I was really scared for the first time that I could remember. I decided it would be best to work more hours in order to stay out of trouble.

Spending time with Karen was a trip, for she had a lot of baggage. She didn't know what she wanted out of life. I was also spending time with Red who was no better. I felt like I was playing with fire, drinking all the time, and getting high. Of course, I thought I was happy, but actually I was just escaping reality.

One weekend, I ran into Karen at Sergio's place. While we were talking, her beeper went off. She called the number and asked me if I would drive her to an address the person had given her. For those who don't know what a beeper is, it was a little clip-on box and had a telephone number assigned to it. When people wanted to get hold of you, they would call the number, and you would hear a beep. Then, you would call them back.

As we were driving, she told me she was a call girl with about six clients. She would give them what they wanted, and with the money she made she could support her addiction. She told me they were all over the age of fifty-five and just wanted companionship. I thought that sounded crazy.

I drove her to a big house on the east side of Midway Road in Dallas. There was a sports car, and a Mercedes Benz SUV parked in front. She said, "I won't be long, maybe thirty minutes." Thirty minutes came and went, and I was left waiting two hours. She finally appeared and apologized saying her client had paid her $500.00 dollars for her services and didn't want her to leave.

Another time, I took her to a home in the upscale Highland Park area. Her client wanted to know who the guy in the car was, so she told him I was her pimp. She always gave me money for gas and then spent time with me.

One day, I called Tom Thumb and told my boss that I was going to be a little late. I was always on time and rarely called in, so he told me to just take the day off. I really needed a day off after escorting her around. I could not believe what I was doing, it was like I was becoming crazy like her.

I spent the whole day with her and the next morning woke up drained from being with her. I learned why all her so-called clients wanted her; the sex was incredible. We had been drinking all night, so I was hung-over. In addition to my job at Tom Thumb I had a part-time job and knew I couldn't go to work. Not knowing what I was going to tell them she asked me for their number. Howard, the manager, answered the phone, and she told him, "Jorge won't be able to work today because I am going to give him a massage." Howard just laughed and said, "That's okay with me."

After a few months, I wanted to distance myself from Karen, her dope problem, and her call girl thing. When we first met, I thought she was cool and had potential. Now I was afraid I might catch something or get caught with her. Fortunately, Karen just disappeared, and I never saw her again. Strange, but I don't know whatever happened to her. She might have ended up with one of her clients or got herself into trouble.

TOTAL DENIAL

I started seeing more of Red. She always gave me space and never questioned me about where I had been. I needed someone at the time, so I started falling for her all over again. She had major problems, and I thought that if we got serious, she would change her ways. So, we decided to start over and even talked about getting married.

I continued to have lots of problems and drinking more, but I managed to stay away from hard drugs and the herb. I still had that empty feeling inside of me. I was the assistant produce manager at the time but was having trouble managing the pressure. I stepped down to be a production clerk and transferred to a different location. I soon realized it was not the job that was giving me trouble; it was my drinking.

However, after a few months in my new position, I was working with a strong crew, doing well, and upper management started believing in me. I was in the spotlight and thought I could manage the produce department again. The attention went to my head, and I started thinking I didn't have an alcohol problem.

So, I drank often, but when I reported to my probation officer, I would deny drinking alcohol. They gave me urine (U.A.) tests every now and then, and I would be told they found alcohol in my system. I always denied it and told them I had taken NyQuil for a sore throat and my cough. They would let me go and encouraged me to drink alcohol-free medicine to avoid a positive test.

Red and I went to an Aerosmith concert and were having a blast drinking. We started smoking weed, but I didn't know why I was smoking it. I should have known better. Soon after, I noticed my lips were numb. The weed had been laced with crack. When

I discovered it, I threw the rest of the joint away, got mad at Red, and left the show. Two days later I reported to my probation officer, who was asked to take a drug test. I knew what the outcome would be; I would test positive. I did test positive but got lucky. They let me off with a warning but told me if I continued using it, I would end up in prison.

The next day, I arrived at work and went straight to the Store Manager office. I told him I needed help, that I had an alcohol problem. It was not easy admitting it, but I knew I needed help. I was afraid of where I might end up and knew I needed to make a change. I did not want to go back down south. I was sent to this facility; it was some kind of hospital in Richardson. They told me that I had a problem with depression, which was the cause of my excessive drinking. I started going back to AA meetings and got sober. They gave me a prescription for Prozac and after being on it for a few months I thought everything was getting back to normal.

The drug really helped me. I was able to work, rest, and live life. Everything was going well, and I hardly ever had negative thoughts. I had been clean for eleven months, and felt like I was living the dream, always positive about everything, and feeling energized.

A VOID – WITHIN ME

I started having a feeling deep inside like something was missing. I was not sure what it was or what I really wanted. The void made me unhappy, and I felt empty. I started to miss the wild lifestyle, and that is when I had my first relapse.

I had been dating a good-looking girl and couldn't get enough of her. She was like Red, cute and wild. I always loved those wild southern women to a fault. We went to a club named Dallas City Limits. I started drinking and was having a blast. After a while I was buying everyone drinks. She got upset at the way I was acting and wanted to leave. I don't remember much about that night, but I do remember standing in front of her car to block her exit. Needless to say, she was upset with me.

Later she told me that if I really cared about her, I would quit drinking and make a change for the better. Unfortunately, I was not about to quit drinking so I told her that if she did not like me the way I was she could hit the road. She did and ended up getting her life together and working things out with her former boyfriend. At the time, I thought that she really did not matter to me because I had Red, and we always had a good time together.

Roxxann Marie Kirtley

LIES AND MORE LIES

Red and I were two wild party animals wrapped up together. Boy, did we ever party. We would get high on dope and stay up all night. There were times we could not have sex because we were too high or drunk. However, most of the time we had good sex and couldn't get enough of each other. We did it everywhere; the park, the lake, and at one of our favorite hangouts which was a dead-end street named Lakemont.

Once again, I started to fall in love with her and gave her all the attention. She loved the time I was giving her and we even talked about marriage. She had lived a rough life and shared everything with me. I was afraid of marrying her because she had areas in her life that I did not like or approve of.

Our relationship was like a roller coaster. About the time she would regain my trust, she would stab me in the back. Like the time she ran off and visited her ex-boyfriend, David. She slept with him behind my back. I found out and chose not to be around her. She was a bad influence. Then, she came running back crying and apologizing, saying she would never do it again. We had sex, and I forgave her and took her back. I guess you could say I was, pussy whipped.

INNOCENT CHILREN

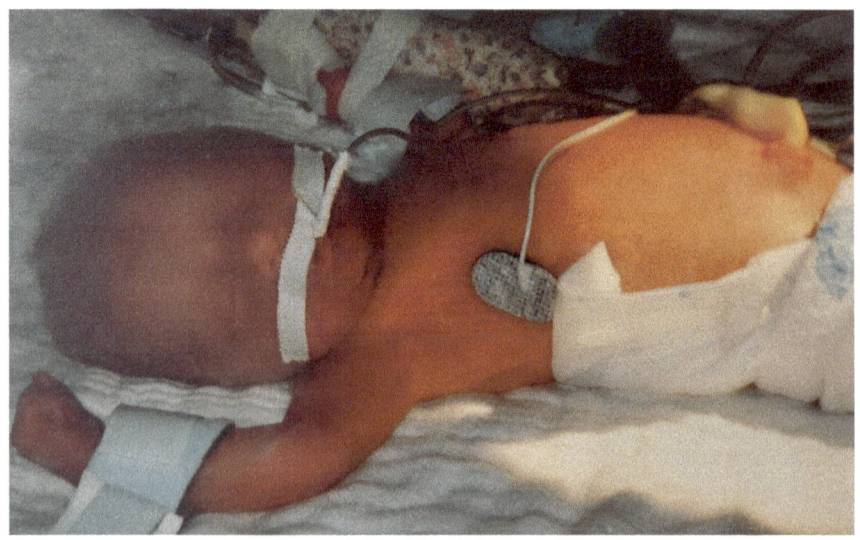

Natali's birth

In March of 1996, Red had a little girl and named her Natali May Camacho. Natali was born prematurely, and she gave her the middle name May because she wasn't due until May and my last name. I was the only other person who came to see the child at the hospital. Because Natali was a preemie, they told Red she would need to stay in the hospital.

Red and little Natali May

Ashley and her cousin

I thought she was my child, but Red told me she wasn't sure who the father was. She said it could be mine or her ex-boyfriend's. I got upset and started drinking, later that day I yelled at her and asked if the child wasn't mine, why did you give her my last name. Red got upset and left the hospital.

THE UPS AND DOWNS OF J.C.

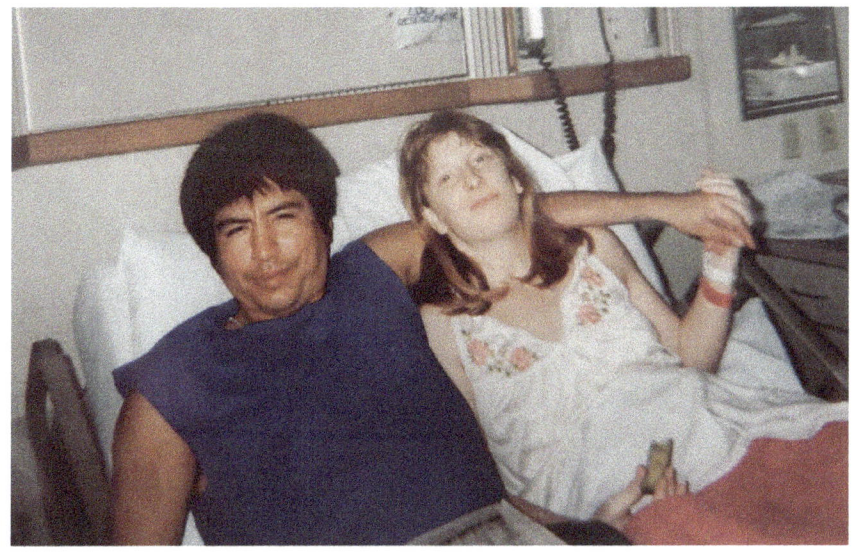

Red and me at the Hospital

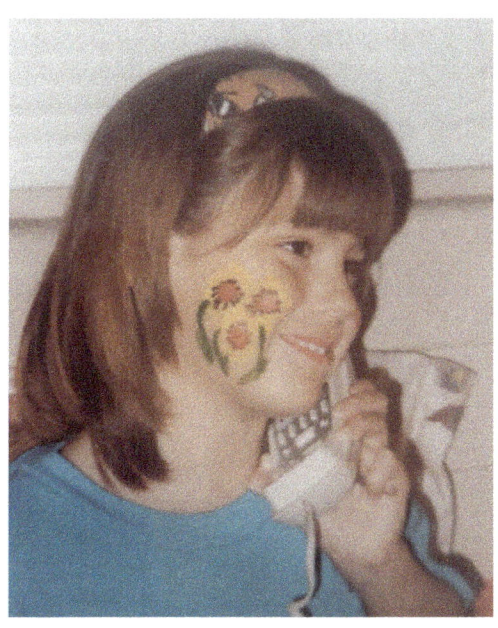

Ashley calling me

I found out that she had started using drugs again to escape her own agony. I cried inside and asked, "God why did she go through the trouble of having a baby if she wasn't going to be there for her baby?"

Ashley and little Natali

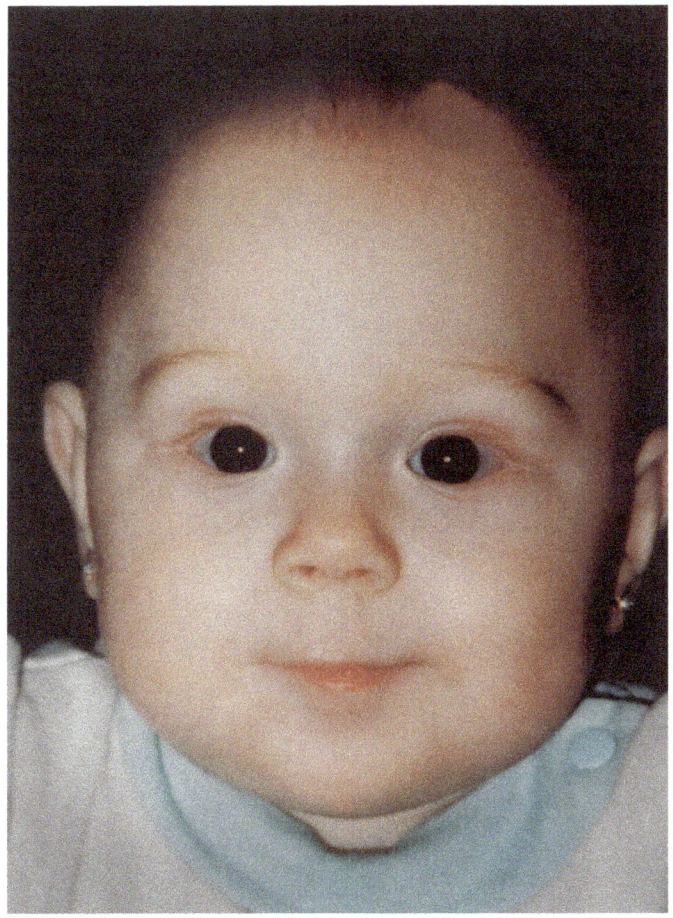

Natali May

I went to see Red's mother, Jo, to let her know that I would care for the child and be there for her. I found her in tears. I asked where Red was staying. She said the hospital had just called and asked if the child's mother was available. Natali was ready to go home. Red was nowhere to be found. I later learned she was staying with her cousin, and when I managed to talk with her, she did not want anything to do with me.

NO MORE TEARS

I thought it was best to stay away from Red for a time because she was going through a lot. She decided to move to Mount Pleasant and live with her grandparents, Haltom and Lois. Her grandparents are wonderful people. I spent some time with them, and they always made me feel welcome. They would cook breakfast, lunch, and supper. With three meals a day, I was always well fed.

Deep inside I was afraid her move was just an excuse to continue using. But I held out hope that she made the move to become more organized so she could care for her children. Well, after a month she called saying she missed me and wanted to talk. She told me I could help raise Natali. She sent pictures of Ashley and Natali. On the back of one of the pictures she wrote, "These are the ones you should love. If you love me, you have to love them as well."

Red, Ashley, and Natali

I did love those precious children and would do whatever to be there for them. I told little Ashley that I was not her real father, but that I was willing to be a father for her. Red and I got back together, and seemingly everything returned to normal. Normal was a relative term considering our normal was not like anyone else's.

Me at the Shell gas station

I'm stocking goods at the Shell gas station

I was still on probation and had to attend my AA meetings. They kept me on course, and I managed to do well and stay positive. I also landed a part-time job at Shell Gas and Oil, a gas station to keep me busy and earn extra money. I knew if I worked, I would stay out of trouble.

I would see Red, and we'd started talking about marriage all over again. I wanted a place I could afford, but she did not know what she wanted. I was not sure that living in East Texas was a good idea. Like before, I was not ready for marriage, and she still wasn't showing signs of being a responsible mother. I feared the outcome.

THE UPS AND DOWNS OF J.C.

A clean Car at the Shell gas station

Behind my back she was still communicating with her ex-boyfriend who was now serving a ten-year prison sentence. She told me that she still loved him. I talked to her and told her that if she wanted to be with me, she would have to cut him off completely. She said she would, but she continued to write to him. She figured what I didn't know wouldn't hurt me.

She managed to get assistance from the state in the form of food stamps and public housing to help care for the children. When possible, I helped any way I could. On my days off, I would go and stay with her, taking plenty of beer, wine, and weed with me. Sometimes, I returned to Dallas with little Ashley because she was enrolled in the Dallas Independent School District (D.I.S.D.).

Little Ashley

Ashley Marie Rice

Bluebonnet picture of Ashley

Ashley Marie Rice

One weekend, I visited, and Red's cousins who were a wild bunch, were smoking weed and partying. They were all younger, and I became curious about what else was going on when I was away. Every time I visited there were other people around.

Out of jealousy, I started accusing her, saying things just didn't seem right. I called in at work and asked for time off so I could spend a few days trying to find out what was going on with Red. I discovered that she was back to her old ways and using drugs.

I wondered to myself, *why am I putting up with this person.* It did not make any sense. I ended our relationship knowing I did not deserve any of this. NO MORE TEARS and NO MORE RED.

Some time passed and as always, she called saying she wanted to see me. It seemed I could not stay away so late one night; after getting drunk I headed to east Texas. It was around 1:00 a.m. when I arrived and there was a guy hanging around in front of where she was living. I asked what he wanted, and he told me he needed some dope. In a heartbeat I ran him off. I confronted her about what was going on and asked why strangers were coming around in the middle of the night. I was so upset I got in my car and headed back to Dallas. I do not know how I made it home, but I knew I needed to get away from her, she was a toxic person. Deep inside, I wanted to care for Natali. I wanted to be her father no matter what.

Ashley Marie Rice

Red and Little Ashley

MY LAST RODEO

Mid-October, in 1996, I was doing well, and my life was better. I thought I had gotten over Red, and I was working on myself to become a better person. I had so much potential, but she was always holding me back.

I had my full-time job at Tom Thumb where I really liked working. Time seemed to fly by when I was there. Some days, it felt like I had only been there for three or four hours, but I was really there for nine or ten hours.

I also still had my part-time job at the Shell station. When working the day shift, I would always stock cigarettes, beer, and other items because at night there would only be one person working. That person did not have any time to do anything but focus on the gas pumps and serve customers inside. I always had fun working there. I knew the area and the people well, and I lived only about five minutes away.

Bike riding

On my way to work one day, I passed by Red's mother's house and Red's blue car was in the driveway. I began wondering if she missed me or wanted to see me. Like many times before, I thought about trying to make things right. The next day as I drove to work, I noticed that the car had not moved; it was still parked in the same spot.

My 1968 Galaxia 500

Red usually called wanting to apologize so I knew something wasn't adding up. I had not heard from her in quite a while. I figured by now I would have heard something, so I started worrying about her. At the same time, I wondered how I had gotten myself involved with a person with so many problems. I just wished she would change and become a normal person and someday be a good mother and a good wife.

The truth was, I was really into her. I cared about her and little Ashley. One day, I was daydreaming and pictured being her husband and we had a few more kids running around. Suddenly, my co-worker yelled, "I got it George." Startled, I woke up from my dream.

I could not get her off my mind. It was like she had some kind of spell on me and knew how to get my attention. In the past she would send post cards and, on the back, would be written, "The spell will never be broken." It freaked me out. We had this so-called love-hate relationship. We were into each other, but her drug use interfered with our relationship.

After finishing at work, I got into my car and headed home. Passing by her mother's house, I saw that the car was still in the very same spot. I thought, *this is crazy*. I was drawn toward the house and decided to go over and see her mother.

I knocked on the door, and little Ashley answered the door. She asked where I had been and told me that her mom was in jail. She could not stop talking and expressed how extremely disappointed she was with me. I told her to please calm down. I cared for little Ashley and loved her very much; she was like my stepdaughter.

Her grandmother Jo came into the room and explained everything to me. Red had abandoned Natali leaving her with some strangers at a restaurant while she went looking for some dope. Leaving Natali with total strangers was unacceptable. How could she leave her child behind? You never intentionally put your child in danger. That was the worst thing a mother could do in my book. I thought about getting her out of jail but kept my thoughts to myself. I was upset and angry at her and felt she deserved to be in jail for doing that to a beautiful innocent child.

I cried inside for many days and when I wasn't working just stayed at home getting drunk. I had her blocked on my phone; I did not want to talk to her. I did not want anything to do with her. But there was little Ashley and now Natali. I thought to myself, *who will provide and care for them if something happens to Red.* I started thinking of a solution. Even though they were with their grandmother, she had health issues, so I would need to prepare just in case.

THE GLASS HOUSE

I started receiving letters from Red while she was incarcerated at the Lew Sterrett Justice Center that we called the Glass House. Mostly, I ignored the letters and would get wasted so I could forget about her, but the letters kept coming.

I finally tried to read some of the letters in the middle of the night when I was drunk. In one letter, she said that hopefully my new girlfriend was treating me with love, respect, and being faithful. In another, she said I was supposed to love her, not just screw her and use her. In another, she asked for a few bucks to help her get cigarettes and a few other things. She said the food was terrible, and she needed to buy something decent to eat.

I felt sorry for her and put some money on her books to keep her happy. In one of her letters, she mentioned that she put me on her visitation list. I knew she wanted me to see her, but I was still upset with her. I did not want to see her. She would get in my head by complaining about everything. I just kept drinking and drinking trying to escape the drama.

The drinking was taking a toll on me. I normally went to work early but increasingly I found myself going to work late and usually with a hangover. I was a total mess!

THE UPS AND DOWNS OF J.C.

Fun at the park

My boss started to notice that there was a problem and that there was something wrong with me. I was losing focus and could not think straight. Everything was off, physically and mentally I was having trouble, and my work performance was suffering. He asked me to see him and asked if I needed some personal time to work on my issues. He was a great store manager who cared about his employees.

At home, my mother asked me what was wrong. Mothers always know when something is off or wrong. I just kept quiet. She told me that I was drinking too much and needed to be careful.

One night, I came home drunk after spending time at a local park by myself. I broke down in front of my mother telling her that my so-called daughter, Natali, had been abandoned at a restaurant by her mother. She did not believe me because I was drunk. The next day she asked me if what I had told her the night before was true. I said yes and that I didn't know how to manage the situation. I apologized to her for my drinking.

I slowed down a lot on my drinking so I wouldn't lose my job. I also wanted to be prepared for anything that might happen. I began working lots of hours and made sure to attend all my AA meetings. I did my best to disguise what I was feeling and continued to deny that I had a problem.

I told my probation officer that everything was going well at home and at the workplace. I lied to her about how I was planning to settle down and start a family. Once my session was over, I would zoom out of her office knowing I was free for another month.

I had been working lots of hours and had checks in my wallet that had not been cashed. Every week, I had been working hard to avoid temptation. I also had been wondering how Red was doing. I decided to cash one of those checks at the Shell station and filled up my tank. On Friday December 6, 1996, around 10:30 I headed to Lew Sterrett. It was a freaky Friday.

Everyone makes mistakes. Even though her mistake was wrong and was not one my family would ever make, I had to forgive and move forward with my life. Anyway, deciding to put some money on her books was the least I could do. I had a good heart.

Before getting on the freeway to head toward downtown Dallas, I decided to stop and pick up a 12-pack of Budweiser and ice it down. I had not eaten much in all the excitement.

As soon as I arrived and pulled into the parking lot, I had second thoughts. I stopped and bought a hot link with all the fixings from a street vendor. Then, I turned the car around and sped out of the parking lot. I stopped at the Hasty Liquor store and bought some more beer; I didn't want to risk running out.

Soon, I was back in my neighborhood.

THE NORTH TOWER

As I cruised through the neighborhood, no one seemed to be around. Apparently, everyone was still working. But as I turned on North Brockbank Drive, I saw a friend, Aaron, working on his truck. I decided to stop and drink a few beers with him. Soon, we were out of beer, and I was starting to get drunk.

I took off for the store to buy more beer where I also got a small bottle of Jack Daniels and a couple of packs of cigarettes for Aaron. It was still early, around 4:00 p.m., and I did not have to be at work until 11:00 a.m. the next day. So, when I returned, we kept drinking and I even smoked a cigarette. I usually only smoked when I was drinking, pretending to be cool and fit in.

Aaron's girlfriend was at the house and offered me something to eat. They were exceptionally good people who cared about everyone. I turned her down and kept drinking. I said I was fine and continued to drink a few more beers. The more I thought about Red the more upset I became and the more I drank. Aaron asked if everything was all right and suggested that I should go home and get some rest. Instead of listening to his advice, I got mad at him.

I climbed into my Baby Blue 1968 Galaxie 500. I had purchased the car from a doctor and had the engine re-done. The car ran so smoothly you could not hear the engine when it was idling. In the back, I installed a sound system using Pioneer speakers and mounted three-way speakers on the front. That car was a real keeper.

I remember I would take the car to the park and just sit and listen to music. People would come near to hear the music. I often wondered if it was the car or the music they liked. Once, at North Lake, one of my friend's girls turned down my music claiming it was too loud. We were jamming to Led Zeppelin and some guy from two cars away said, "Honey you never turn Led Zeppelin down." So, I cranked it up, and we all jammed together.

I sat in Aaron's driveway and let the car run for a while. I took some Tylenol P.M. thinking by the time I got home; I would be ready to hit the restroom and then go to sleep. Then, I would wake up around 8:30 with plenty of time to get a shower and grab a bite to eat. Anyway, that was my plan.

Well, that plan never happened. Right before I got to the intersection of Merrell Street and Brockbank Drive, I fell asleep at the wheel and hit a parked car. I hit my head on the rearview mirror and my knee on the bottom part of the dashboard. I could not believe what I had just done. Suddenly, a man ran out of this house where the car had been parked and started screaming, "What have you done?"

He headed straight for me, and I panicked. So, I jumped out of the car not really knowing what to do and started running in the direction of my house. I left everything in the car including my keys and wallet. The clothes I had just picked up from the cleaners were hanging in the back. Being intoxicated I fell a few times.

The house was only two blocks away and my little brother was out front working on his truck. He had no clue what had just happened. He could tell I had been drinking, so he told me to go inside and get some rest. Unfortunately, I didn't listen to him because I was drunk and stubborn, conditions that get you into trouble.

It wasn't long before a police car pulled up, and one of the police officers called me over saying he wanted to ask me some questions. I responded right away telling the officer I did not know anything about the accident. Two officers immediately got out and approached me. Dummy me, I had just given myself away because neither of them had asked about an accident.

They inquired about the blood on my face and knees. Initially I told them that I fell. It is unbelievable to think that I was going to be able to lie my way out of this situation. All the evidence was in the car that was registered in my name. Running from the scene of the accident didn't go over very well. I should have listened to my little brother and gone inside to sober up.

An ambulance showed up, and EMTs treated my wounds. Then, the two police officers took me into custody, and we headed to jail. This time, I was taken to a new jail called the North Tower which was nothing to be proud of. The North Tower building was an addition to the Lew Sterrett city jail so they could house more inmates.

The North Tower

After a few days being there, my older brother and father came by to see me. My wonderful father cared for all of us deeply and always went out of his way to help us. Such a great father to have. But I always let him down by not taking his advice. He knew I liked to party and told me if I had to party do it at home where I would be safe, and no one would bother me. I felt ashamed being locked up.

Frank Crowley Courts Building

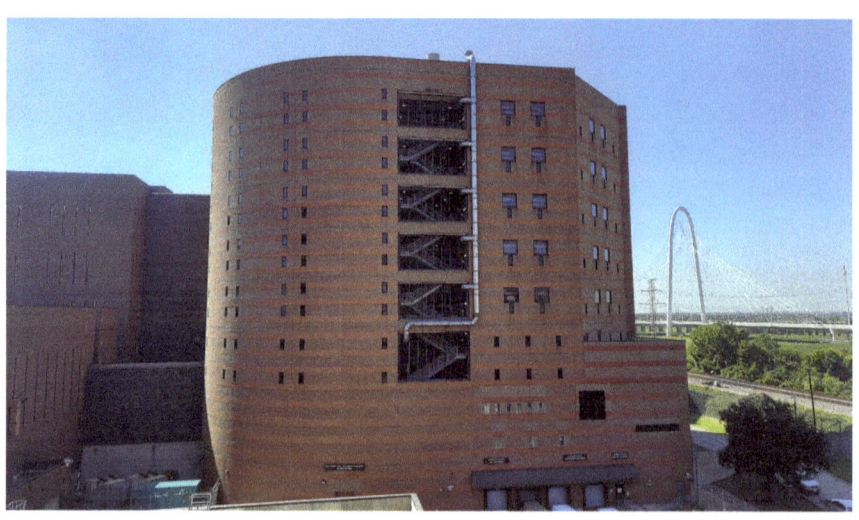

The North Tower

I asked them what had really happened. I had been having nightmares where someone was screaming, and little children were crying. At first, they didn't respond, and I thought I had done something terrible. Then they told me that I ran into a parked car and was acting like a fool. Thank God, I was relieved to hear there was no one in the car. When you blackout there is no-telling what could happen.

Praying to God

Well, my kind father didn't like seeing me in jail and offered to bail me out. I told him not to bother. Since I was on probation, the court would just return me to jail, and his money would be wasted. I reported the accident to my probation officer and waited to see what the outcome would be.

It was not long before Red got wind of what had happened. Now, we were both in jail, I could not believe it. She started sending letters and critizing me. In one of her letters, she said that I had just proved to everyone what a drunk I was. Her letters upset me, and not wanting to be the recipient of her venom, I ignored them. In fact, I blamed her for everything.

Justin Adam Camacho

In her next letter she dropped a bomb on me. She was six months pregnant, and it was my child. I thought here we go again. She told me that if my family did not fork over some money, she was going to put the baby up for adoption.

I was so angry at her that if she were standing in front of me, I think I would have slapped her. Of course, I never would, but I sure thought about it after reading her threat. But I didn't trust her and couldn't believe what she was saying.

Knowing that she was having sexual relations with other men and not using protection, I wrote back and asked how she knew the child was mine. She said a doctor friend had given her a shot that would keep her from getting pregnant. She said I was the last person she had slept with before getting the shots.

She was driving me crazy. Around the time she got pregnant, she was partying but mostly with cousins and a few friends. I knew for sure that I was the only person she was having sex with. The child had to be mine. She found out it was a boy, and I told her I wanted to name the child. She agreed, saying it made sense. I told her to name the precious baby Justin Adam Camacho.

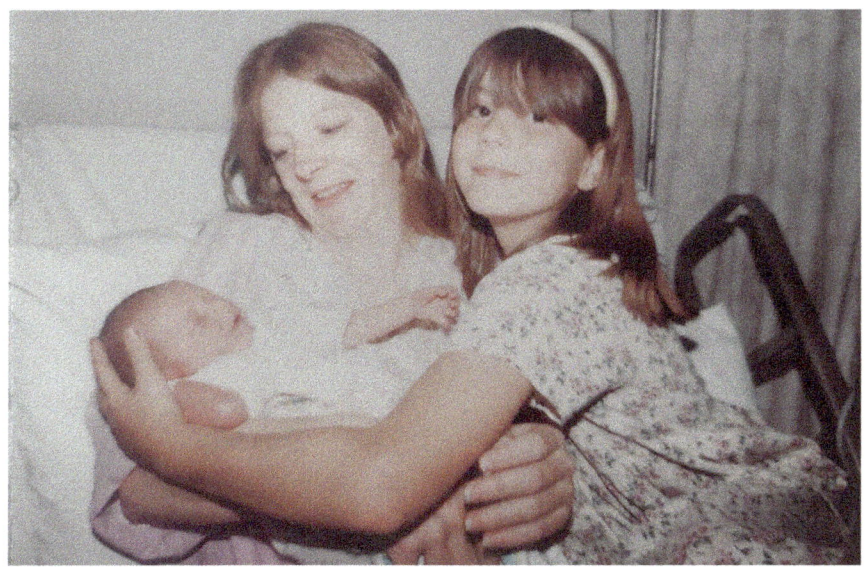

Red, Justin, and Ashley

The authorities said she could go free on one condition: she had to attend a rehabilitation center for six weeks to deal with her addiction. Two weeks later she was out of jail, but still pregnant.

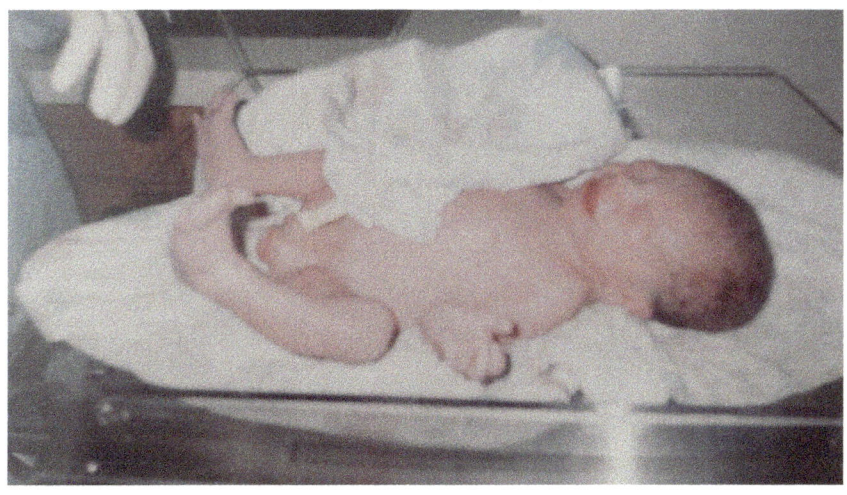

Justin's birth May 12, 1997

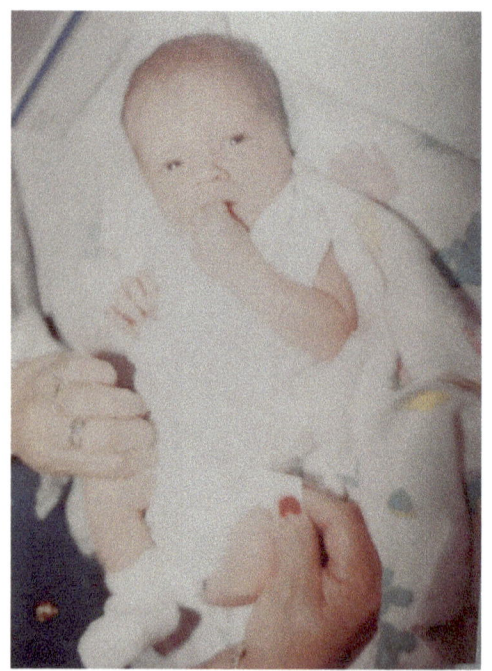

Justin Adam Camacho

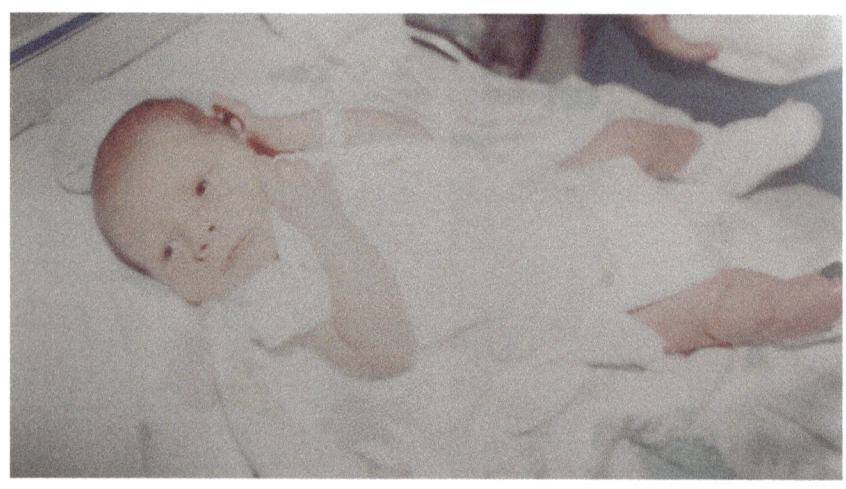

Justin Adam Camacho

We kept up with each other, and Justin was born on May 12, 1997. Not being able to attend the birth of my son was a total shame. Red told my family she wasn't sure I was Natali's father, but she knew for sure I was Justin's father. Justin is 100% Camacho. Fortunately, my mother and sisters were there. Mother brought my newborn little boy to visit me at the North Tower. I couldn't believe what a beautiful baby he was. We were separated by security glass, but he kept moving his tiny little hand as if he were trying to touch me. It was like my blood trying to reach out to me. I could tell by his hair and eyes that he was my son.

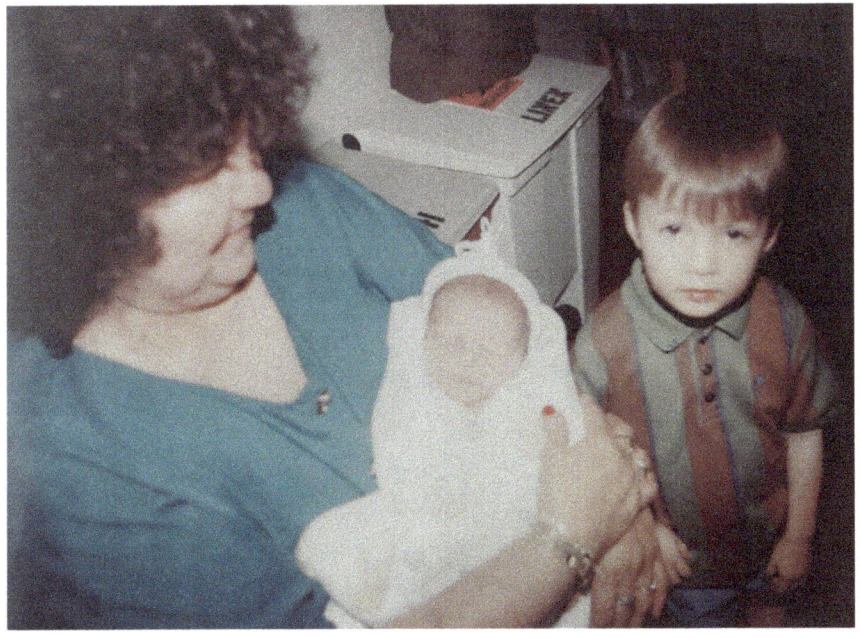

Mother, Justin, and Matthew 1997

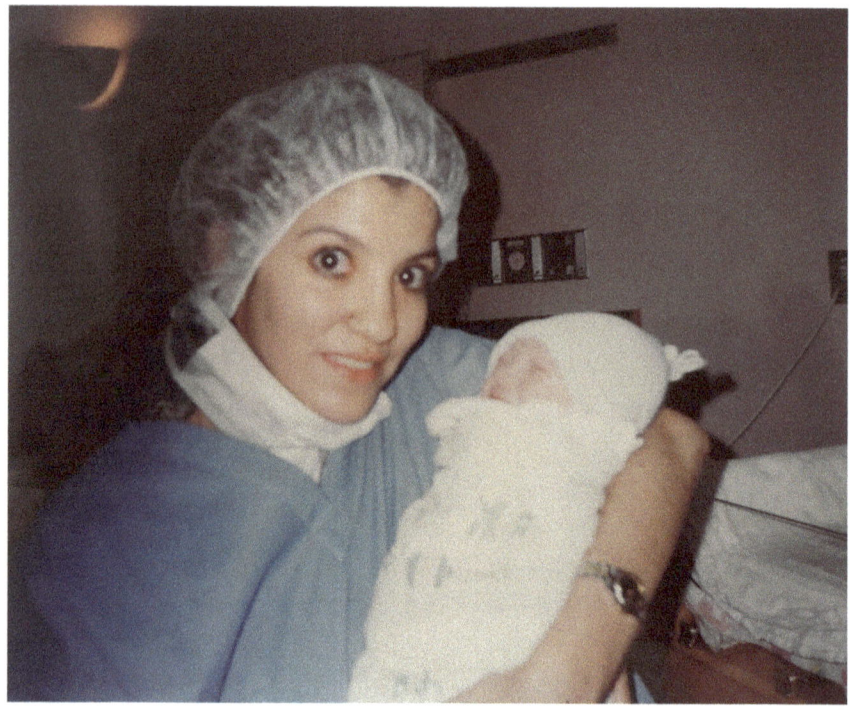

My Little Sister Mary and Justin Adam

What a wonderful feeling. One time, my mother came to visit and broke down and started to cry. I never liked to see her cry, not even when I was young and in school. She told me that something was wrong with little Justin. I asked what could be wrong with such a beautiful and healthy-looking baby. I thought she was going to say he had an infection or some disease. Then she stunned me, at the hospital they had found traces of cocaine in his system. He also was born with a bad eye and had to be operated on.

Red had been using during her pregnancy. I was so disappointed but did not know what to do given my current situation. The fact was, there was nothing I could do, not a darn thing. I had sleepless nights thinking about how she was using drugs while knowing she was pregnant. I was driving myself crazy. I thought, what a sick person, *why did I ever get involved with her?*

Like it or not, I was involved now more than ever. There was no way out of this situation. For many days and nights, I cried out asking why she couldn't wait to use drugs until after the child was born. My family thought the same thing. Now, Red's life continued on the outside while mine continued behind prison walls.

M.A.D.D.

Red came to visit me once, while I was in jail, but she seemed to be in a hurry to leave. She looked like she had been up all night. I knew what she was doing, but I refused to accept her lifestyle. When I called her at home, she would tell me she was fixing supper for the family. I would get upset and jealous that I couldn't be there. I thought there might be someone else, and she did not want me to know. I figured she was cheating on me, but I refused to let go! Well, I told myself, what I don't know won't hurt me. What do I do now? I loved her, and I really did not know why. It was that spell she had on me.

Mothers Against Drunk Drivers (MADD) were protesting inside and outside the courthouse. They didn't want anyone with a D.W.I. to get a light sentence so they pushed for the maximum sentence for every offender. I could understand because a lot of the offenders had killed innocent people. MADD wanted justice for the families and loved ones of those killed. I could have done the same, but thank God, I didn't kill anyone. They seemed crazy and had me worried. I was sentenced to five years in prison on June 26, 1997. I deserved what I got and thought it was fair. Actually, I received a lighter sentence because I did not hurt anyone. If I had injured someone, I would have gotten more time.

M.A.A.D.

M.A.A.D. demonstration

CHAPEL SHOCK

Before my sentencing hearing, something happened that had nothing to do with how long I would be locked up. I ate chow early, and on Sunday mornings I noticed people going to the chapel. As they passed by, they would say, "Camacho, come with us to church." I had no clue how they knew my name. I responded thanks but no thanks. They just smiled and shook their heads.

I started having strange dreams where I heard a little voice say, "Go!" In another dream, I saw Jesus flying west across the sky, and many angels were on either side of him. I remember thinking it was like they were going to war. I was looking up and then looking down. I felt the jailhouse shake, and the jail was cracking in half. All the inmates were falling, and some were begging for mercy, asking God to forgive them of their sins.

I woke up in a cold sweat and thought to myself, *it was just a dream*. Two days later, I had another dream. I could not see anything, but I heard that little voice again saying, "Go!" It sounded so promising, unique, and trustworthy. The next day was Sunday, and I was so determined. I was going to the chapel no matter what. I didn't care what anyone thought.

I got up early and took a shower. I paced back and forth, while one of the guards just looked at me. Soon, I saw some prisoners heading to chapel. When they saw that I was joining them they looked at me and smiled. One shook my hand, and another said, "Welcome." As we got closer, I started to feel different. As we entered the room, I noticed people praying and speaking in tongues. Feeling nervous and afraid, I stood close to the back wall.

The reverend or pastor as some called him thanked everyone for coming and gave an opening prayer. I closed my eyes and started to pray, asking God to please protect my family and to bring them comfort and understanding. I sensed something filling my entire body; it was like a high I had never experienced before.

The harder I prayed the higher I got. The high I was experiencing was an unbelievable feeling. I felt like there was a magnet on the ceiling making my hands rise up into the air. I felt a strange string of light move from my elbow to the palm of my hand and felt something come out of my hand. It was the most amazing feeling I had ever felt. I cried out saying, "You are real Father Almighty. Please forgive me."

I had hurt so many people in so many ways. I heard the same voice that told me to go, telling me that my time here would pass and that I would be fine. Suddenly I felt a strong hand touching my hand. I thought a brother had come to pray with me. I opened my right eye to see who it was, but there was no one around. I still felt that powerful hand touching me.

After the service, I called my little sister, Mary, and told her that everything was going to be fine.

DEEP DREAMS

CATCHING THE CHAIN - THE BLUE BIRD

The time had arrived for me to be transferred. The personnel had notified us the night before who would be "catching the chain." I waited patiently until we were escorted one by one according to jail procedures and boarded the blue bird.

The BlueBird

Criminals were seated two per seat on the bus, taking us to the T.D.C. unit to which we were assigned. I was about two rows in front of the back on the left side. I could see the anger, frustration, and fear on the faces of the men. There was so much talk about the South and how inmates were being treated. I did not join the conversation because it was supposed to be a sign of weakness. Some fell asleep, some made noise, and others just stared out the window.

1978 THE ICE STORM

I dozed off and entered a wild daydream. I visualized the crazy fans attending The Texas World Music Festival in the summer of 1978. Everyone was having a blast listening to the bands, taking in the environment, and even enjoying the Texas heat. I walked down to the floor and watched Journey while they played one of my favorite songs, Wheel in The Sky. They were impressive and amazing.

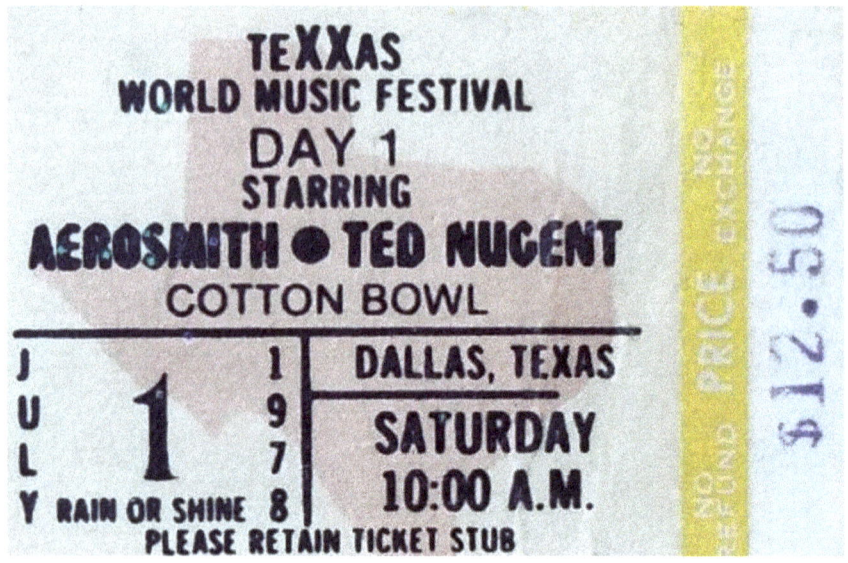

My ticket stub for the TEXXAS Jam

HEART Playing the "Magic Man," photo by Roy Reyna Jr.

Cheech & Chong at TEXXAS Jam 1978

TEXXAS Jam poster 1978

Photo by Roy Reyna Jr.

THE UPS AND DOWNS OF J.C.

TEXXAS Jam, photo by Roy Reyna Jr.

Nancy Wilson, photo by Roy Reyna Jr.

I was surprised because they were not even supposed to be in the line-up. The festival was being held at the Cotton Bowl Stadium, which was packed with over 100,000 fans. A few of the bands were: Van Halen, Eddie Money, Heart, Head East, Ted Nugent, Atlanta Rhythm Section, Frank Marino & Mahogany Rush, Aerosmith. I remembered getting to see *Cheech* and Chong as well. They came on stage before the next band would play and were so cool. I was drained watching everything, so I headed toward the lower balcony and found a seat. That's when the famous song "Dream On" was playing and the whole stadium lit-up with Bic lighters. It was an amazing sight! I reached for my camera to get a picture, but I had run out of film.

I witnessed some of the best bands of all time. Van Halen was just beginning and had everyone on their feet cheering and next came Heart and their popular hits were impressive. Somewhere I got some film and managed to take a few pictures of Heart, Journey, Ted Nugent, *And* Van Halen, but the pictures were blurry, because it was like a swamp down on the field. The moment is what counted the most; it was my first festival ever and it was amazing. The Texas Jam that year would be my first festival. From that year on I attended every Texas World Music Festival held in the Dallas Cotton Bowl through 1988.

THE UPS AND DOWNS OF J.C.

Van Halen Rocks the Cotton Bowl

Van Halen Rocks the Cotton Bowl

Journey at the TEXXAS Jam, photo by Roy Reyna Jr.

Van Halen Rocks the Cotton Bowl

THE UPS AND DOWNS OF J.C.

The Wilson's Sisters Rock the Cotton Bowl

1978 TEXXAS JAM

HEART at the 1978 TEXXAS JAM

Cooling off at the 1978 TEXXAS JAM, photo by Roy Reyna Jr.

THE UPS AND DOWNS OF J.C.

Enjoying the music

Ted Nugent at The Cotton Bowl

Following that summer came the Ice Storm of 1978, which was one of the most intense storms in Texas history. After the extreme summer heat, the cooler weather was a welcome change, but no one was ready for what was coming. Dallas County lost power, schools closed, and temperatures dropped into single digits. Many were left without power for over two weeks, and deaths were reported. I remembered that winter, I was young and wild, and it was an amazing time for me.

Mom, Alma, and Mary in 1978

THE UPS AND DOWNS OF J.C.

My precious two little sisters Alma and Mary

Alma and Mary Camacho making a Snowman

Mary E. Camacho in 1978

Jesus O. Camacho in 1978

Jorge A. Camacho in 1978

My older brother Beto and two siblings

My little Nephew Nuno and me

Suddenly, I was shocked back to reality when the bus came to a roaring stop. We were dropping off three inmates at the Coffield Unit in Prison in Tennessee Colony, Texas. We could feel tension in the air. It was freaking wicked, for we could also feel death in the air.

SUMMER OF 1979

I felt the bus moving forward and soon found myself in another daydream. This time I was attending the Texas World Music Festival in the summer of 1979. The headliner bands were Boston, Heart, Van Halen, Sammy Hagger, TKO, and Blue Oyster Cult. I remember seeing bodies all over the floor of the Cotton Bowl. It looked like a war zone, something you would see in a movie. It was hot and people were exhausted; some even passed out.

I remember Heart playing in the evening during a misting rain. I was in front of about ten rows from the stage. It was epic to see Ann and Nancy, the Wilson sisters. It was a blast listening to Van Halen, who was spectacular, and Nazareth, which was the band I grew up listening to. I owned most of their albums.

TEXXAS JAM 1984

HEART, a Great Band in the early 1980s

Ozzy 1984 TEXXAS JAM

THE UPS AND DOWNS OF J.C.

Jake E. Lee 1984 TEXXAS JAM

Alex Lifeson of RUSH at the 1984 TEXXAS JAM

MONSTERS OF ROCK AND TEXAS JAM

As we continued to travel the movement of the bus put me in another deep sleep. This time, I was attending *The Monsters of Rock* in 1988. However, I woke up when everyone started yelling aloud when the ride got really bumpy. I wondered what was happening. It turned out that the bus was having an issue with one of the rear tires. The driver had pulled over so the tire could be either repaired or replaced.

We waited, and after a few hours, a truck pulled up and performed the necessary repairs. By this time, it was dark, and no one had any idea where we were heading. I just knew we were heading south.

TEXXAS JAM 1988

THE UPS AND DOWNS OF J.C.

TEXXAS JAM ticket stub 1988

TEXXAS JAM t-Shirt 1988

I fell back into another deep sleep. This time I was attending the last Texas Jam being held in 1988. I remembered seeing *Metallica* playing during the day. There was a swamp of hard-core metal heads dressed mostly in black cheering and enjoying the songs. I was sitting on the upper balcony, and they were playing the song *Ride the*

Lighting. In the distance I could see a storm heading towards the stadium and there was lighting in the clouds. Freaking wicked!

Suddenly, my dream took me back to the 1985 *Texas Jam* featuring *Deep Purple.* I was standing on the floor about twenty rows from the stage. *The Scorpions* started playing *Rock You Like a Hurricane* and the crowd went crazy; people everywhere were pushing each other. Rick Medina, a great friend of mine, was standing behind me and holding on to my shoulders while people were moving back and forth like waves. It was insane and formidable! Everyone was soaked in sweat. Rick and I were in the middle of it all. Even *Ted Nugent* put on one heck of a show. Those were good times I thought to myself.

TEXXAS JAM 1985

Grim Reaper 1985 TEXXAS JAM

The Scorpions 1985

THE MASTER

I woke up and couldn't go back to sleep. To pass the time, I thought about my first job working for Safeway Food Stores. I worked for them from 1976-1986 and it was a great company. I gained a lot of experience there and worked everywhere in the store. I had a lot of flexibility because I only lived two blocks away. In 1986, Safeway decided to close their doors, so I took a few days off. Needing to stay busy and earn money I went job hunting, and a Tom Thumb Grocery Store hired me immediately. I began in the produce department where my experience helped. Of course, with a new store, there might be other ways of doing things. I quickly became familiar with their program. Store # 40 was located at Forest Lane and Marsh. 1986 went by fast, and in 1987, I was promoted to third man status. They gave out titles just to keep employees happy.

The Produce Merchandiser saw that I had potential and kept coming around asking for me. Also, my Produce Manager did not want to lose me to another department. They were holding me back from getting promoted, which created some friction between the boss and me. I almost quit but decided not to. I continued at that store through 1990 when I was pulled to help at the district level.

They sent me to different stores to do re-sets and other displays. I was like a floater. The job was different, and I had a lot of fun. I worked hard and for many hours. I was ready for a change, and they offered me the Assistant Produce Manager position in 1991. I took courses to enhance and develop my skills: Effective Communication, Customer Relations, The Complete Manager, and Produce Management and Operations, which was my favorite. I was now more than qualified.

My first assignment was to work with one of the Produce Managers helping him run the department. Later I was sent to store #5 and worked under Mr. Joe Martinez. If Joe did not know how to do something, no one did. Joe saw something in me. I had great people skills which he admired and considered important in retail. He taught me how to make money for the company in many ways.

The MASTER and me

Joe Martinez

Joe would take me to eat at Herrera's Mexican Food which was next door to our store off Maple Avenue and Denton Drive. What an amazing place to eat. It was a popular place, and all kinds of people dined there. It was always busy and full of people, especially on Saturdays. There he poured his wisdom into me.

Manny DeLa Cruz and cousin Joe Martinez

I owe Joe for showing me how to set up the Produce Department with color breaks and other visually attractive ways. But the most important thing he taught me was how to get co-workers to work for me. He told me that if I wanted to gain their respect, I must treat every person the way I wanted to be treated. I learned having the right approach was key and especially important. It was okay to push people to work hard, but you didn't want to shove them. You always wanted to thank them for everything, even the petty things. A simple Thank You goes a long way.

This amazing person was more than my boss or co-worker Joe was the Master. He took me under his wing in the early part of my career and taught me so much about life. I was promoted to a higher volume store due to his mentoring. He stayed in touch and would come to visit me at other stores. He treated me like family and the son he never had. I knew I could trust him. He was like a father figure to me.

Joe, Virgina Martinez, and family members

Julianna's sweet Sixteen preparations

Joe Martinez and Grand Daughter Julianna

THE UPS AND DOWNS OF J.C.

Joe and Tom Martinez

Joe Martinez and Family

Joe Martinez was the Master in the category of displays and won many contests over time including Manager of the Year.

Joe Martinez awards wall

Joe Martinez, 55 year award

Current images of the Martinez family

Older image of the Martinez family

STATE JAIL

We finally arrived in Palestine, Texas, at the Gurney Unit on July 23, 1997, where I was assigned. I went through the entry process and filled out all the paperwork. I was told that if I acted right and got involved in all the programs offered, I could be out in about 18 months. Half of my sentences were thirty months, so I was ready to toe the line.

I was at the Gurney Unit for a month when they informed me that I was being transferred to the Hutchins State Jail. Hutchins was only about forty minutes away from my home, and I was allowed to have two to three visits per month. I also had a friend from the old neighborhood who was doing time at the unit.

Unbelievable to me at the time, I ran into Red's ex-boyfriend David. He surprised me one day as I was heading to the chow hall. He reached out and offered his hand. I shook it, and he said, "Welcome to the family." I was part of his family now because he was Ashley's father whom I had treated like my step-daughter. Of course, she hated me at times for being with her mother.

Hutchins was okay, but I learned immediately that if you were not strong and did not defend yourself, you would be considered weak, and other inmates would take advantage of you. One time, I got in this younger guy's face and called him out. By doing so I earned everyone's respect.

There were all these youngsters wanting to test someone; it was like a game to them. You would be surprised at what you can learn in just a small amount of time so, I was always ready for anything that might happen. I learned quickly how things operated at the unit.

I hung around my same people, La Raza (my race). They were always there for me, and it seemed like no one wanted any trouble with us. I also spent time together with the guys who were transferred with me, and I tried to help the ones who had nothing.

TEAM OF THE 1990's

I watched all the football games, and yes, I loved watching my team, The Dallas Cowboys. I always supported them no matter how they were playing. Win or lose, I will always be a Cowboy's fan.

THE UPS AND DOWNS OF J.C.

I remember when the boys were tough, and no one could beat them. They kicked some butts. Watching Super Bowl XIII in 1979 against the Pittsburg Steelers was a tough one. The Cowboys almost won it, but Jackie Smith dropped a pass from Rodger Staubach in the end zone. The highlight of that play will haunt me forever.

Go Cowboys 2006   Dooms Day two defense

 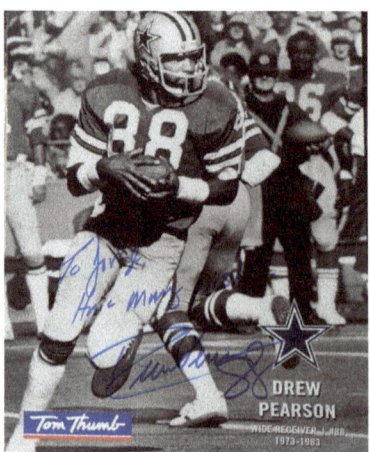

Hall of Famer Drew Pearson #88

Cowboys for life   *The legendary Tom Landry*

I stood with them in 1989 when Jimmy Johnson replaced Tom Landry and went 1 and 15, their only win coming against the then Washington Redskins. That was a bad year. I stood with them through the good times too when they were considered The Team of the 90's. In 1992 and 1993, they won back-to-back Super Bowls against the Buffalo Bills. They would have been the only team to win five Super Bowls in a row had it not been for the incident owner Jerry Jones created with coach Jimmy Johnson in 1994.

Team of The 1990's

To Jerry's credit, in 1996 they were able to get revenge on them ole Pittsburg Steelers by beating them 27 to 17 in Super Bowl XXX. Oh, I should mention that it was the Cowboy's fifth Super Bowl overall. Anyway, watching football on Sunday's made my weekends fly by.

I tried not to think about Red or the free world, which is what we inmates called outside the prison walls. Anytime I saw David, her Ex, it reminded me of her. At times, I would go crazy and was not doing my time right. Time was doing me, which was insane!

One Wednesday, I was told to turn in all my books that I had checked out to read. After eleven months they transferred me to the Holliday Unit near Huntsville, Texas. I had been expecting my family that weekend but figured they would understand.

MY FAMILY

I arrived at the Holliday Unit on Thursday pretty drained and tired from traveling. Anyway, on Saturday morning my new cellmate, Tom, told me that someone had come to see me. I ignored him and went back to sleep. Then he told me that if I didn't want to see my family, I could refuse the visit.

Little Justin, Matthew, and me at the Holiday Unit

Justin Adam and me at the Holiday Unit

At first, I thought I was hearing things or dreaming about what he was saying. But I got ready, shaved, brushed my teeth, and put on some deodorant so I would smell decent. I followed their normal procedures and passed through this door to the visitation area. I could not believe my eyes. Mother, Dad, and little Justin were there waiting. They had driven five hours just to visit me. I did not show it, but I cried inside, for I was so happy to see them. My family tried many times to encourage me with good advice on how to live my life. Even though I didn't respond correctly, they knew I was hurting and continued to support me and stand by me. Mother and Dad cared for the most important person in my life, my little Justin Adam Camacho.

I was blessed to have this kind of family. Where were all my so-called friends? The ones who said that if I ever got in trouble or needed help, would they be there for me? They were nowhere to be found!

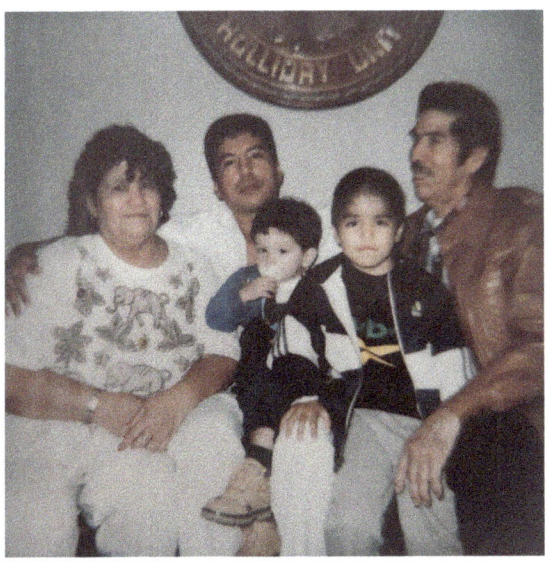

My wonderful family visiting me at the Holiday Unit

The voice within me

However, I had one devoted friend, Gilbert Orozco, who offered his help. I consider him a friend for life. Thanks, Gilbert, for checking on me and for being there. My mother always spoke highly of you. I offer you a sincere Thank You. I really appreciate your caring attitude.

When my family came to visit, little Justin did not know who I was. He would look at me strangely. Whenever Mother or Dad went to get me a snack or drink, he got scared. They were familiar, and he would wonder where they were going. At that time, I was just a stranger to him, which was understandable.

Gilbert and Anna

I told my family they were welcome to come once a month, every other month, or when it was convenient. I also told them not to come if it was raining or cold. I did not want them to risk a wreck or get sick. I let them know I would be fine.

My Father and his three daughters

They visited every four to five weeks and brought snacks and pizza. It didn't take long for the pizza to run out. What a treat, just beautiful. A whole fresh pizza enough to feed four grown men. I took pictures with and for them and always kept one for myself. Every time they came, I would think about the hurt and troubles of my life. I was convinced of my stupidity and was sorry for the pain and suffering I had put my family through.

Back in my cell at night, I would cry out to my Lord, "I will change my ways. Please let me out so I can be with my loved ones." That is when I decided to start working on myself. I started getting seriously involved in the AA meetings and took other classes that could help me work on my path to recovery. Some of the programs helped me a great deal.

But, to tell you the truth, another reason I was motivated to start taking classes was to cool down because the rooms were air conditioned. During the summer months, when the heat was brutal. I would do anything to avoid working in the fields and avoid the bosses who were not nice whatsoever; they treated us badly. Yes, I still had to work, but only in the morning when it was cooler. Having a good motivating reason to attend was helpful because the more I went the more I heard things that hit home, and I began learning about dysfunction.

Another reason for staying away from the work fields were the snakes. The bosses told us they were their pets. Once I saw an inmate scream and started running because he had encountered a snake. He was heading toward a boss on horseback and almost got shot. The boss said, "Boy what are you doing?" They took him to the Black Cave, which was a place for individuals who couldn't get along with regular inmates or had committed a serious crime inside the system.

The bosses were just doing their jobs, making sure we knew what would happen if we acted up. They wanted it to sink in so we would behave. If someone continued in their old ways, they were going to pay one way or another. They could also find themselves doing more time and, in some cases, many more years. I knew they had machinery to do the field work, but our jobs weren't about the work; they were about punishment. Sure, they still benefited from the work we did while being punished.

I.N.S. DETAINER

I learned that I had been transferred to this unit because they had an immigration hold on me. Everyone went through a background check, and the authorities wanted to know if someone had other names or aliases. They wanted to know if they were United States Citizens or had been born outside the United States.

At the time, I wasn't considered a U.S. citizen even though I had filed for citizenship before I being incarcerated. I just never inquired, and I didn't receive anything informing me of my status. I didn't think it was that important. Well, I soon found out how important it was and learned that I was under investigation.

I was being investigated for everything from my past. There was a law passed in September 1996 which allowed the authorities to deport any person who posed a threat to society. I fit into that category, and they were implementing the proper proceedings to have me removed. I had a felony conviction on my record stemming from the two D.W.I.s I was charged with in 1994 and 1996.

I was allowed to speak with the State's Counsel in the unit at no charge. They were trying to make me sign a specific piece of paper which I refused. The person started asking me many questions about my past. Heck my name had come up in other parts of the country; California, Nebraska, and parts of Nevada. It was crazy because I had never lived or visited any of those states.

My family secured an attorney for me. The authorities started asking if my parents were citizens of the U.S. and if so, did they become citizens before I turned eighteen-years old. Even though my father was born in Gregory, Texas, I still had to go through the removal proceedings. I went to court many times. They asked for proof that my dad had been born in Texas. He had always lived in Texas even before I was born. We showed them his birth certificate and proof that he was enrolled in school in 1938. That still wasn't enough evidence to exempt me from the removal process. Nothing made any sense: I had lived in Texas most of my life and had adapted to the American way.

Come to find out they had confused me with another person who was using my identity as his own. Everything was put on hold.

I kicked myself for not having taken care of my legal status a long time ago. When I was in high school, I signed up for the draft and almost joined the Army. I remember that my older sister and brother asked me if I wanted to go with them to take the test to get citizenship. I said, "No thanks."

Partying and girls were more important back then. I figured I was already in the U.S., so what could go wrong. I had many opportunities to take care of my status and had failed to do so.

THE LONG ROAD BACK

I was blessed to be in the best part of the entire unit with the trustees and those who had been designated as SAT II. These were the ones that behaved well and were getting close to their release date. There were still fights here and there, and the Unit would get locked down for assorted reasons. But mostly no one wanted any trouble; we just wanted to go home.

As for me, I went from the hole squad to the garden squad. I managed to go to all my meetings and found myself going to church about six times a week. The unit provided everyone with something to do, and it was up to each individual to take full advantage of what was being offered.

I had a desire and wanted to change and live a different life, so I made the decision that I would take full advantage of what they had to offer. I did not want to return here ever again. I had hurt my family too many times, especially my mother. I did not want her to suffer any longer for my stupidity. I had let everyone down.

I was on my way up again, and this time I was determined not to ruin my opportunity by denying my drinking and drug problems. I started to pray for everyone in my family, for my known enemies, and the enemies I didn't know about. I prayed for peace in the world. I prayed for Red and her beautiful children Ashley and Natali. I asked God to help with her drug addiction. I asked Him to wake her up so she would realize her wrongdoing and be a better person for her children. I prayed and prayed, which was all I could do from inside. That's when I started doing my time instead of the time doing me.

I started to accept things, and something strange happened: I started feeling at peace. For the first time, I felt like the void in my life was starting to be filled in. I did not know what was going on, but I began sleeping better, and my time started to fly by.

TOXIC

The only time I would get upset is when Red would write and tell me how much she loved and missed me. Then, as I started thinking about our days together, time slowed down again, and sleepless nights returned. I was letting her get into my head again. I did not know what to do and thinking about her drove me crazy.

I would receive letter after letter, and then, she would unexpectedly stop writing, which was very upsetting. I wrote back and told her if she was going to write and then suddenly quit writing that I'd rather she quit writing all together. I considered what she was doing as a type of punishment. She always wrote back with some excuse for why she had stopped writing. Eventually, I ignored her letters.

Deep inside, I knew she was back to her old ways. God confirmed this knowledge by giving me dreams where I could see her doing dope all by herself in what seemed like a bathroom. She was also having sexual relations with other men. God was trying to show me what kind of person she was. He was allowing me to see her for what she really represented in my life. I had always refused to believe or accept that she was toxic to my life.

The Lord knew the direction I was heading and that if I went back to my old friends and behavior, it would be only a matter of time before I hurt or killed someone drinking and driving. I would end up in jail again and be facing a whole lot of time in prison. My family would suffer the most!

THE SPELL WAS BROKEN

I sat in my cell thinking, "NO... NO...NO!" That is the moment when I started to lose my love for her. I had finally faced the reality that I had to move on and let her go.

Her spell on my life was like a revolving door. I would show her love–she would do me wrong–I would accuse her–she would say she was sorry–she would promise to be faithful– I would forgive and take her back. The door kept spinning with me in it. All the while, she was lying to me.

I had no concept of love or being with a person who was truthful, faithful, and supportive. Someone who would seek help to fight their addiction if for no other reason than to be there for her children. Someone who would not ignore her problems and leave her children alone to suffer.

I continued to work on myself. I found out that to help others I first had to help myself. I accepted who I was, what I had done, my assigned prison time, and the environment is was in. I had to make the best of where I was and not let it get to me.

I attended various meetings like AA (Alcohol Anonymous), N/A (Narcotics Anonymous, and E/A **(Emotions Anonymous)** where I shared my feelings with everyone in attendance. I let my anger and frustration out when sharing. It was part of the recovery phase that everyone goes through. After every meeting, I felt better. I was also going to church.

The more I thought of myself being in prison the more I embraced the reason God had allowed me to spiral out of control. Everything started to make sense. I started to forgive others even the people who had punished me, Police officers, judges, friends, and Red. She was the toughest one for me to forgive. But the spell was broken. I did not love her anymore; instead, I committed to pray for her.

THE VOICE

The day after the spell had been broken, I read some writing that was on the wall in my cell, "I am here for a reason. I am not here by chance, but by God's choosing. His hand formed me and made me the person I am. He compares me to no one else—I am one of a kind. I lack nothing that His grace can't give me. He has allowed me to be here at this time in history to fulfill his special purpose for this generation."

Holy Dove

From that day on my time started to roll by a little faster. One of the guards notified me that someone wanted to speak with me about a replacement job. They escorted me to an office and a prison representative asked If I was interested in working in the commissary. I did not hesitate to say, "Yes." I knew it would be like working in a convenience store, and it was air conditioned.

The only negative about working there is that we got strip searched before starting work, whenever we left to get something to eat, or when we returned to our cells. Regardless, I enjoyed working in the commissary because it made my time go by faster. Having a decent job helped change my appearance and I hoped that would lead to reducing my time.

MY JOURNEY OF LIFE CONTINUED

My hope for a shorter sentence was taken away in November of 1998. I was set to be paroled on February 7, 1998. I was just four months away from release when the Parole Board met and I received a Set-Off, meaning they were denying my parole and would not consider the matter again until September 1999.

Their decision caused a horrible feeling, like someone had hit me in the stomach and I couldn't breathe. I responded by attending daily AA and NA meetings and church activities. I considered the setback a test thinking, *no worries, it hurts, but there is nothing I can do but press on.*

However, I was more concerned that my family might think I had done something wrong and was being further punished. I agonized over how to explain the situation to them, especially mother! I did not want to be the one to break the news to her, so I wrote a letter to my sisters explaining what had happened in the hope they would tell her. The good Lord knows how much grief I had brought upon her.

At my next AA meeting I talked about how hard it was to let my family know about the issue. The advice I received was difficult to hear but freeing, "You need to tell them in person." The next time my mother and father came to see me, they brought little Justin and my little niece, Celina. I told them what had happened and explained the new law which had passed which allowed them to make me serve my entire five-year sentence. Letting them know in person was not as hard as I thought it would be, and I felt better knowing they learned the news directly from me.

They took the news great and asked if there was anything they could do. They were ready to hire an attorney to help me get out sooner. I told them that hiring an attorney would be a waste of money, that I had gotten myself into this mess and was working to become a better person. I said we just needed to let things take their course and see what happens.

Sadly, I was still a stranger to little Justin. During our visits he really liked being in front of the camera so my parents would take a bunch of pictures. Justin just smiled. I looked at the pictures for days before putting them in my photo album.

Once, when they came to visit the unit was locked down and they had to return home not knowing why. I wrote to them letting them know I was okay, but that the unit had been locked down for safety reasons, which was true. Actually, someone figured out a way to sneak a pistol into the unit and took a T.D.C. officer hostage. I couldn't tell them the real reason, or my letter would not have been delivered.

Meanwhile, I learned that I.N.S. was still investigating me. The following week I learned that I had a court date in four months and that I was being transferred to another unit. I had caught the chain once again, but I had no idea where or why. I packed my belongings and started saying goodbye to all my friends.

Before I was set to board the bus the authorities said I would be heading to Hondo, Texas southwest of San Antonio. Instead, we drove to the Limestone County Detention Center in Groesbeck, Texas east of Waco. Limestone was a transfer facility for the overflow population and housed some federal inmates. The unit was actually much better than any of my previous units: it had air conditioning and telephones. The best part was it was only about an hour and a half from Dallas.

Upon arrival, I called home and spoke to my little sisters, Mary and Alma. I told them I had been released and they needed to come pick me up at the Greyhound Bus Station in downtown Dallas. I could hear the excitement in their voices, as they yelled, "We will be there in a little bit." Boy, it was a good thing they did not hang up, I was just pulling their leg. Man, they would have gathered up the family and made a trip downtown for nothing. I thought it was pretty funny, but they weren't too thrilled. Anyways, I laughed and told them that I would be on my way out soon enough.

ESTOY SOLO

I still wondered why they had sent me to the Limestone Unit. There were people I knew from DFW and some I had been locked up with at Dallas County and other facilities.

There were a lot of Raza (my people) there. One of the homeboy gangs was called the Tangos and they provided protection. People joined so no one would pick on them. Fortunately, it was up to each individual to join or not. I let them know that I was solo; I did not run with anyone. I let the Tangos know that if anything bad happened I would always be loyal to my Raza. They understood and respected my position.

One time, a so-called gang member wanted me to join his family, and I told him I was just a short timer passing through and respecting everyone. I told him I knew a lot of people at the unit that were my family. He got upset and said, "You're the one that usually gets taken." I knew I could defend myself, so I told him that if he gave me any trouble I was going to cave in his nose. I stuck my full fist remarkably close to his face. He stared at me like he wanted to fight, and I said, "Just you and me, not me and five of your family." He was a chubby little person, and I knew I could do some damage.

Guys like him only act brave and like to fight when they are surrounded by their little gang. He asked me to meet him outside in the recreation yard. He was trying to set me up so his gang could jump me and force me to join them. I told him I was not scared of him and that if he did not settle this right away or back off, I was going to make him look bad in front of the one who "carried the keys." That's what the gang leaders who oversaw their organizations were called.

I let him know I wasn't alone. My friends from the old city jail came up and stood with me just in case they were needed. He got scared because I stood up to him. Realizing what he had gotten himself into he responded, "Never mind, forget the whole thing."

I spent most of my time drawing envelopes and in the recreation yard walking and jogging. I also had a friend from Puerto Rico, and we would meet in what was called the flex yard where we could throw horseshoes. I enrolled in a Life Skills Training and took a Substance Abuse Class. I also attended church twice a week. I really enjoyed the church services at this unit. I wanted a change in my life because I was just sick and tired of the direction my life had taken.

There were always free-world people as we called them coming that came into the units and praising God with us. They sacrificed personal time that could have otherwise been spent with their loved ones. There were three loving ladies in particular we all enjoyed: Joyce, Laura, and Frances. These ladies enjoyed serving the Lord and spreading His word. They brought us doughnuts, orange juice, and beautiful cards for us to send to our loved ones. They always led us in praise, and we appreciated them for hosting our church services and keeping us company. Everyone was grateful for their service.

I constantly prayed to my God asking Him to give me back my freedom. I also thanked him for protecting me and sending me to the Limestone Unit. I knew that there were rougher places than this one.

ROCK BOTTOM

In the summer of 1999, my parents came to visit with my little troublemaker, Justin, and he couldn't wait to see me. The door of the waiting room opened, and he started running toward me, and that was the moment I realized he was really my son. His blood was calling out to me. I always had a certain feeling when he came to visit, just like the time when I was in the City Jail, and he tried to touch me through the glass. This time with no barrier to separate us he ran into my arms. It was a surreal moment.

From that visit on, any time he came to see me I picked him up and carried him around the room. He loved being in my arms. Visiting time was short, only lasting about twenty minutes. Our time together flew by in a flash and then he would be gone.

Later, I would look at the pictures we had taken and cry out to God, "Why do I have to go through all of this?" Deep inside, I knew the answer; so, I could overcome my addiction, get stronger, and become the responsible person God longed for me to be. My heart ached, and I cried inside about all I had put my family through. They didn't deserve the consequence for any of my actions.

Previous unknowns started to make sense to me in many ways. I was on the road to recovery, my journey from rock bottom. I needed to be strong so I could finish the journey. I sensed that there would be better times ahead that I would get to share with my boy and my family.

Things were moving right along until I started thinking about the free world. Those thoughts slowed down my time, and my journey would begin to stall. It was natural for me to long to be free, but I had to resist thinking about the outside world and maintain focus on the work inside I had to accomplish.

I prayed for God to guide me in and through the hardest and deep areas of my heart that needed to change. Calling out to Him made me feel better and I wanted to do the work necessary to improve. Of course, God answered the prayer by allowing me to be tested by facing the temptation of doing wrong. I thought, *not this time*. Instead, I surrounded myself with good people who were on a similar journey and who were thinking positively. I did not want any trouble; I just wanted to go home.

CATCHING THE CHAIN TO HEAVEN

Two years had passed, and I knew it wouldn't be long before I would be catching the chain and sure enough three weeks later, I was sent to the Holliday Unit for the second time.

We arrived on a Wednesday, and I was assigned to the F building where I found some of my old friends. I was even reunited with a remarkably close friend. I visited the Commissary where I used to work and said hello to all the people who were still there. I bought a few things and headed back to the dorm where I asked God to surround my loved ones and me with his Angels.

I began attending church at the unit and experienced something new. All the time that I had been going to church, I was afraid to join the crowd and cry aloud asking the Lord to come into my heart. Oh, I had said the words in front of a few people but had always been reluctant. One day I broke through the pride standing in my way and I cried out in front of everyone, "Lord Jesus, I need you. Thank you for dying on the cross for my sins. I open the door of my heart and life and receive you as my Savior and Lord. Thank you for forgiving me and giving me eternal life. Take control of the throne of my life and make me the kind of person you want me to be. In Jesus precious name. Amen!"

I felt better knowing I was heading in the right direction. I had caught a different train, this one led to Heaven. A feeling came over me that someone was looking over and blessing me from above. I felt peace inside, and that night I slept well.

THE ROLLER COASTER CHAIN

Soon I caught the chain and was returned to the Limestone County Detention Center and was assigned to J Building. After all the time I had served, I finally got a bottom bunk bed. Unfortunately, it was only for a week because I caught the chain to the Byrd Unit, which was considered a diagnostic unit.

Ashley, Natali, and Justin

Justin's 3rd Birthday

On the bus as I looked out the window, I saw a neighborhood with small houses and nice trees all around. I noticed a little boy riding his bike and playing with his friends. My mind drifted off, and I wondered about my little Justin and how much fun we would have if I were out there with him. I thought about all he had been through; the eye surgery and having his father in prison. I realized that I had not heard from my family and that started to bother me.

Family visiting me at the Byrd Unit

While at the Byrd Unit unexpectedly, Red started writing to me again. I couldn't figure out why, but I wrote back. I shared my experience on the bus about seeing the boy riding his bike and how it reminded me of little Justin. I wrote that my cellmate always looked forward to me talking about Justin because he always loved having kids around. I shared how we could relate to each other. I'm sure she thought I was losing my mind. I believe the Lord was softening my heart in preparation for me to enter the free world.

My cellmate and I saw a dove nest on top of the fence surrounding the facility. Two doves would come and go so we figured they were taking turns sitting on eggs. One would stay on the nest while the other searched for food. One day, we noticed there were two little birds in the nest. They had broken out of their shells and were being fed by their momma and poppa.

One day, the momma bird waited and waited for the poppa bird to come back with food. The momma bird started to fly away but nervously returned, never going more than a foot or so away from the nest. There was no sign of the poppa dove, something had happened.

Not wanting her babies to starve, the momma dove decided to take off in search of food. After a while, one of the baby doves got frustrated and managed to climb out of the nest. The little bird fell to the ground and hit the concrete; it was killed instantly. The other baby dove did the same but landed in the grass and started wandering around. Soon the bird found the shade of the building shielding it from the sun.

There was nothing we could do given our situation. We knew it wouldn't be long before the little bird would starve or be eaten by a prey, maybe a cat. About thirty minutes later, the momma bird returned to the nest. She looked both ways, but there were no signs of her little loved ones. In her dove voice she cooed, crying out for her babies. She obviously didn't know whether to look down or she would have seen where they had fallen.

My cellmate and I shared the ongoing adventure with the other inmates. They were all eager to know what ultimately happened to the dove family. I told them that the momma bird found and rescued her loved one. Though I knew that wasn't the case, I wanted to provide a positive outcome to give them hope for a better outcome.

Some days passed and I learned that I had caught the chain and was headed to the Goree Unit in Huntsville. My cellmate was a person I knew from my time at the Holliday Unit. I was only at the Goree Unit for about ten days when I found out they were sending me to the Walls Unit. I had no idea why, but usually people were not sent there unless they had a health condition or were going to be released.

I had not heard from my family in quite a while and was feeling lonely. So, I penned a letter to let them know I had been sent to Gorree, the pre-release Unit. Fortunately, I hadn't mailed the letter because two days later I caught the chain again.

Of course, no one told me anything, I just went with the flow. Five of us were loaded into a small van heading east. All these thoughts were going through my mind: *Could it be possible I was on my way out? Maybe I was going somewhere under an I.N.S. detainer. Maybe someone made a mistake, no T.D.C. never made those kinds of mistakes.*

We arrived at the Billy Moore Correctional Center in Overton, Texas, around 10:00 or 11:00 a.m. on August 18, 1999. We were told that it was a great unit that housed less than five hundred inmates. I was surprised that the officers talked to us and treated us with respect. They were kind, unlike the officers at other facilities where they yelled at us for no reason.

I was assigned to A-Pod, and my cellmate was a Christian. He was on the bottom row, and I was on the top row, A-2-28-T. He offered me some of his food even though I could get things at the commissary and could survive off the food from the chow hall. I listened to his radio. I was in a good pod.

Occasionally, a few people came by to say hello and ask if I was riding with anyone. I would simply say, "I ride Solo." They didn't pressure me but usually responded, "If you ever needed anything or help of any kind just holler." There were some good people at this unit.

NO, NO, NO

I shot out some letters to my family letting them know where I was. Red continued to write telling me she loved me and wanted me to come by when I was released. I wrote back and tried to tell her, but she just didn't understand; I wasn't going back to her.

I started thinking to myself, *what am I doing here, why aren't I on my way home?* I felt pride taking over again, so I asked my God to continue to protect me and my family.

I had signed over my parental rights to my mother and little sister. I wanted mother to have full custody of my little Justin so Red could not try to take him from my family. Red agreed that Justin would be better off with my side of the family. We were afraid of her actions and didn't like what she had done to little Natali. For his safety, Justin would stay on our side of the family no matter what. She was not fit based on her past mistakes to be a good mother. She told me that she would like to see him from time to time, if possible.

There was NO, NO, NO way I wanted to go back to my old ways ever again.

HORSESHOES

It was September 1999, and the holidays were approaching fast. After a couple of weeks of getting comfortable at the unit, I signed up for a vocational trade class, Custodial Maintenance. The class was fun and kept me busy. I also continued my normal routine of jogging and playing basketball.

My wonderful family

Summertime 1999

Knowing I needed to stay focused on my recovery, I attended AA and N/A classes and went to church a couple of times a week. I knew if I did not get it together here it was going to be harder to succeed out in the free world.

Justin and siblings 1999

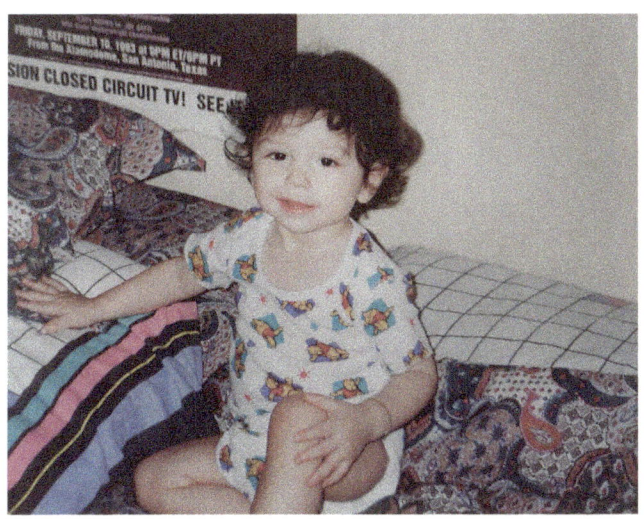

Little Justin 1999

One of my friends at the unit named Otero, and I decided to enter a horseshoe tournament to kill time and have some fun. Let me tell you, it was a tough competition. We lost our first round, which landed us in the loser's bracket. From that point on, if we lost twice, we would be eliminated from the tournament. After that first round, we never looked back. We won the next round and stayed alive.

Horseshoe Champions 1st Place

```
TDCJ - INSTITUTIONAL DIVISION
       OFFICIAL LAYIN PASS
            EDUCATIONAL

EFFECTIVE DATE: 09/22/1999
FROM-TO TIME: 18:00-20:00
START DATE: 09/22/1999  END DATE: 09/22/1999

ADMIT: 00791798 CAMACHO, JORGE ARMANDO
REASON: HORSE SHOE        HOUSE: A-2-38T

JOB: FULL-TIME STUDENT              07:00-14
EDUC:



COUNTROOM: DUNCAN

TITLE: COUNTROOM
```

Horseshoe Tournament Pass

Guess what? The guys that beat us in the first round also got beat, so we got a chance to play them again. They won the first game, but we won the second game 21 to 12 to tie the series. The third game was wild and came down to the wire. The score was 18 to 16 in our favor, but they threw a ringer. My partner was disappointed because it appeared that we were going to lose to them again.

I was determined not to let that happen. I was down to my last two horseshoes, but deep inside, I got this feeling like I had been there before, and we were going to win. My third horseshoe landed close to the post. They threw their last horseshoe and everyone including my partner thought the match was over. Some watching started to walk away. I flung my last horseshoe into the air hoping for the best. As it started its descent excitement began to build and incredibly the horseshoe landed on top of their ringer! We won the game! We went wild but acted like good sports and told them how good they were and what a great game they had played.

That the match could have gone either way, but this time we prevailed to everyone's surprise. Even Otero couldn't believe we had won. This allowed us to continue playing in the overall tournament. We knew that if we threw the shoes like we had that day, we could beat anyone.

On September 15 we won again, but the competition was more difficult. Otero climbed to the top and were in second or third place, I can't remember which. Well, we decided we wanted to go all the way and were not going to settle on anything but first place.

On September 22, we made it to the final round and easily won the first game. The second game was much closer but wait for it…we won! We had come from behind, but in the end accomplished our goal and won it all. I was so happy and just enjoying the moment when Otero yelled out, "We did It, we did it!"

Everyone celebrated our victory.

LIVING LIFE IN THE PODS

About two weeks before Christmas, I shot out about seventeen Christmas cards to family and others who were close to me. I wanted to make sure the cards would make it before Christmas.

In my pod on Christmas Day, all the Spanish people gathered together, shared a big meal, and celebrated Christmas. Afterward, we watched the football games. The Cowboys beat the New York Giants that year and made the playoffs with an 8 to 8 record. Unfortunately, they lost to the Vikings the following week. The St. Louis Rams surprised everyone and won Super Bowl XXXIV on January 30, 2000. The final score was 23 to 16.

February rolled around, and the second day of the month was my last day in the Custodial Maintenance class. I continued going to AA and N/A meetings and stayed in shape exercising and playing basketball. Two weeks later I signed up for a Food Service Class that was starting on February 16, but unexpectedly I caught the chain and was told I would be going to see I.N.S. again. I wasn't gone long returning on Monday February 28 and the trip was fruitless. I had no idea where my case stood.

In March my parents, my little nephew Po yoyo, and my little troublemaker Justin came to visit. I was so happy to see them and felt blessed having a family who loved me. I always thanked God for that.

Mr. Mike Barber and his partners came to minister that month, and it was always a blessing to see them. Mike Barber Ministries is a faith-based ministry that enters prisons and shares the gospel with incarcerated men and women. He was incredible. Spring Break was just around the corner, and we got locked down again for the normal shakedown. We went back to school on the 21st, and everything was returning to normal.

The Pods - being locked down

I was assigned to a different Pod, F where I would meet my crazy cellmate. He was always getting in trouble. Regardless of how he was acting and all the negative people around me, I kept my cool and acted right. I went to school, went to meetings, and attended church. But I was always faced with the temptation to do wrong.

RENEWAL

On March 11, 2000, I was watching television and clipping my nails in the dayroom. One of Mike Barber's ministry team came over and spoke to me. We talked about life and the way I used to live, the direction I was heading, the opportunity being incarcerated provided, and the fact I was rescued from the destruction that was waiting for me. He prayed with me, and I re-dedicated my life to Christ and decided to start all over again. I thank God for allowing that to happen to me.

On April 5, 2000, I turned thirty-eight years old. I did not say a word, but a friend of mine was going to celebrate his birthday on the 8th of April, so I just pitched in and helped make a big spread for the two of us that weekend.

My attorney sent me a letter stating that I had to be in court May 4, 2000. I told my teacher that I would be gone for a few days, but I was back the next day, which was a Friday, so I missed the Cinco de Mayo feast.

Justin's 3rd Birthday

Justin Adam 2000

My little Justin's birthday was on May 12, and he was going to be three-years old. Oh, how I wanted to be there to see him blow out his candles, eat his cake, open his gifts, and most of all to see his smile. I cried inside and felt bad about not being there with him. I told everyone in my meetings how I felt and told them to get their lives together. I told them, "The ones that suffer the most are your parents and family. Especially your mother! You need to start doing positive things in life so you can stay out of places like this. I know there are lot of ways to enjoy life without using drugs and alcohol, and I'm personally doing all that I can to live that kind of life."

In the next few meetings, I opened up more, letting the men know I had come a long way. I was becoming more patient and was just being myself. I was able to relax and sleep better.

The Food Service Class I was taking was about to end. I needed a break and decided not to enroll in the Electrical Class because it required a lot of math, and I was not good at math. I also wanted weekends off. The people in the kitchen wanted me to join their crew, and, at first, I said yes and then decided not to. I did not want to gain weight. I talked to the teacher at the Electrical Class, and he put me on the waiting list.

MY BABY PIE OF THE WORLD

I was expecting a visit from my family on July 1, but no one showed up. I was sad, but figured the weather might have been a problem. To my surprise the next day, Sunday July 2, mother and my little Justin came to see me. My sister-in-law was with them, but she was not on the visitation list. When I saw the two of them, I felt a tremendous joy rise up inside of me like always. It was a beautiful feeling.

My Baby Pie of The World and me

Justin and Freddy at Six Flags

Justin's 1st birthday *Justin's 2nd birthday*

Justin Adam and me at Hurricane Harbor 2005 *Another birthday*

Justin and Natali *Justin at Six Flags Over Texas*

Justin's 3rd grade class *Justin's 4th grade class*

Justin Adam and me

My little brother Pepe and Justin Adam

Justin's favorite toy

Little Justin Adam

Justin Adam, Elsa, and Mary

Bike riding time for Justin

After their visits, I would cry inside, not just because of where I was, but because of what had taken place in my life. I thought about my past and the times I almost died. I knew that I was extremely fortunate to be alive. In the years past I thought I was lucky, but now I knew without a doubt God's Holy Angels were protecting me. That is when I began to see my family differently than before: mother, dad, my older sister Elsa, my little niece Celina, my little nephew Po yoyo, and of course my little Prince Justin, my baby pie of the world. I had previously felt the love of God in me, but never like I was at this moment in time.

Justin Adam and me at the Batman movie

Haunted house at E.D. Walker Middle School

Justin at 3 years old

THE UPS AND DOWNS OF J.C.

Justin taking a break at the circus

Justin Adam and me January 2002

I started the Electrical Class on July 29, 2000, and had a burning desire to continue my education. On the outside I had always been too busy or out enjoying myself to take life seriously. I didn't spend much time worrying about anything except where I could go to get a cold beer or some Jack Daniels. Of course, the drugs also called my name.

At church, I kept asking God to forgive me of all wrongdoing. In AA, we all learn from *The Big Book,* which was written in 1939. I was working on one of the steps that is part of the recovery process. I needed to face all that I had done and the fact that I should have listened to those who loved me when they were trying to help. I started making amends by writing to my little brother and other family members to tell them how sorry I was for everything I had done to them. It was August, and I sent my mother a happy birthday card and told her how sorry I was and that I loved her.

THE CRAZIES

I was living in D Pod at the time and befriended my cellmate. He seemed to be very familiar with filing release paperwork, so I asked for his help filing a motion that could help me get released.

Unfortunately, he was a fraud and soon caught the chain and was moved to another facility. The next cellmate they assigned me complained about everything. He also caught the chain and moved out. The third guy assigned to my cell was completely crazy.

He thought the system had planted a chip in his ear. He would stay up late at night looking out our window. At one point, he said they were shooting at him with a laser gun. He started soaking his sheet, blanket, and extra clothes with water at night and hung them around his bunk to protect him from the people who were after him. One day, he stuck a piece of pencil lead in his right ear in an attempt to remove the chip. His ear started bleeding, and he had to go the infirmary. He told one of the bosses that someone had planted a chip in his ear, and he wanted it taken out. The boss determined he was crazy, and he was transferred to Sky View for the mentally ill.

My next cellmate worked at night and many times kept me up at night. When he returned to the cell, he would turn on the bright light regardless of me being asleep. He would invite his home boys to our cell who had unpleasant habits. One night he woke me up, and I caught him and his friend eating peanut butter and jelly sandwiches. I never did anything to disrespect anyone, but decided it was time to have a little chat with him. Afterward, he started to respect me more, but I sensed trouble.

One early morning, the lady from the mailroom and a Lieutenant came to our cell and said they were looking for something. They wouldn't say what they were looking for, but I figured they were looking for contraband linking my cellmate to a gang. He had tattoos all over his body and wore a lot of blue.

They trashed our cell, damaged some of our commissary goods, and accused us of having extra clothes. Oddly they found some kind of cheese by the vent in our cell. He was the one with extra sets of clothes but didn't say a word in my defense. As a result, they took some of my personal belongings, thermal t-shirts, boxers, and other items. They wrote both of us up and opened a case against us.

I filed a grievance against them, which did not help at all. They ruled against me and gave me thirty days cell restriction. My cell restriction began on August 22, 2000, and ended on September 19. They assigned me to a three-person cell in E Pod, and once again I got the top bunk. I was able to continue going to school, and my counselor gave me a pass so I could go to N/A and AA meetings. However, they wouldn't let me out of my cell to go to church, which I considered most important. I didn't understand why or how they determined my guilt, but that's what happened at times on the inside.

FIRST GRADUATION

I was looking forward to my first graduation from the Foodservice class I had taken. The date was September 23, and I woke up early to get ready. I hoped that my family might attend but had no idea if they would be allowed.

The ceremony started, and my group was called second. They led us out, and to my surprise my mother and little sister were sitting there with her newborn baby, Madison. Then my heart leaped as Justin jumped up and started running toward me. My mother quickly grabbed him saying, "No, you can't go." You should have seen his little face; he was so disappointed. I waved at him and told him it was okay and to wait.

After the ceremony, we were released to sit with our families in the visitation room, which was air conditioned. Refreshments were provided, and I had a lot of fun holding Justin. I expressed how much I loved and missed him. Everyone in the room came over to say hello and told me what a gorgeous son I had. Two of the teachers even took pictures of us. I thanked God for giving me such an incredible day, one I will always remember.

BACK TO NORMAL

Life in the pod returned to normal, but I had missed the first three Dallas Cowboy games that year. Dallas lost their top receiver in the first game and had not been playing well. Redemption came on September 17 when they beat the Washington Redskins on their own turf, final score 27-21. Washington was one of their biggest rivals. In October, they won a game against the Carolina Panthers in overtime 16-13.

A friend, who was from Corpus Christi, made some Halloween envelopes and gave me a few that I sent to my nieces and nephews. My little brother sent me sixty dollars to spend and a note saying he wanted me to buy something worth having. I bought some Rhino boots and running shoes.

November rolled around, and we were locked down for four days, the second shakedown of the year. Mother came to see me along with my older sister, my little niece Celina, and my little Prince, Justin. Although I was in prison, life was good.

THE BIG BOOK

I was determined to follow the Big Book and work on my program. I was on step ten and knew I needed to focus on what I had done to others and to myself.

The Big Book

1. We admitted we were powerless over alcohol — that our lives had become unmanageable.

2. Came to believe that a Power greater than ourselves could restore us to sanity.
3. Made a decision to turn our will and our lives over to the care of God as we understood Him.
4. Made a searching and fearless moral inventory of ourselves.
5. Admitted to God, to ourselves, and to another human being the exact nature of our wrongs.
6. Were entirely ready to have God remove all these defects of character.
7. Humbly asked Him to remove our shortcomings.
8. Made a list of all the people we had harmed and became willing to make amends to them all.
9. Made direct amends to such people wherever possible, except when to do so would injure them or others.
10. Continued to take personal inventory and when we were wrong promptly admitted it.
11. Sought through prayer and meditation to improve our conscious contact with God as we understood Him, praying only for knowledge of His will for us and the power to carry that out.
12. Having had a spiritual awakening as the result of these Steps, we tried to carry this message to alcoholics, and to practice these principles in all our affairs.

Taking my own personal inventory was difficult. I knew the suffering that my mother was going through. I could feel her pain, and it hurt, especially knowing I was the source. My stubbornness and stupidity had landed me in prison. But I thanked God for allowing me to be caught because I knew my experience here would make me a stronger and more responsible person in the future.

I did my best to distance myself from anyone negative and hung around only good and positive people. I consistently went to church and to my N/A and AA meetings. I kept my faith intact and prayed that God would bring Peace to all the men in the unit and that we could have good relationships with one another.

There were times I could feel the tension in the air. I could see and feel the friction all around. That was always the time some bad thing was about to happen, like a big fight or riot. I wanted to avoid any negativity and stay alert.

My cellmate was a Christian and a clean person even though he cursed all the time. There were many so-called Christians here as well in the free world who would say one thing but do something different. I knew we were all hypocrites at times, I sure was, but I also knew that no one was perfect. My cellmate was no different, and we got along well.

He would clean our cell three to four times a day; he was a cleaning fool. I understand he cleaned as a form of exercise and staying busy. One day, he was transferred and was gone in an instant. We didn't have any forewarning, and to this day I don't know what happened to him. I don't know if he had caught the chain or had been released and was going home. I knew his release date wasn't scheduled until March of 2001.

I got another cellmate. He was pretty mellow, but he had a lot of anger inside and told me he hated the system. I did not want to get on his wrong side, so I prayed for him all the time. Knowing he had been through tough times and was paying a consequence for past mistakes, I figured I could learn from him. We talked about our lives and how we could all become more responsible and live a much better life.

Mother and Justin Adam 2001

Justin's birthday party

I would always open up to my cellmates. Getting to know them helped me know if they would take care of our cell in my absence. I always looked out for them when they were gone. I always kept a lock on my locker, not because I didn't trust people, but because of past events. Some cellmates would go through your locker and help themselves with whatever they wanted or simply mess up my things. I liked my things kept orderly and in their proper place.

One time, a cellmate wrote to a family member saying he was my friend, but he tried to scam me. As a result, I developed the habit of always protecting my belongings, so if something went missing, there was no one to blame but me. I encouraged my cellmates to do the same.

The holidays were fast approaching, so I shot out about twenty Christmas cards to my loved ones. On December 23, my father, mother, little sister and her child Madison, and my little prince and troublemaker, Justin, came to visit. I hadn't seen my father in a while, so it was great spending time with him. I loved seeing everyone and especially getting to play with Justin. He and I had a lot of fun.

Mother was doing an excellent job raising him in my absence. She had taught him to speak Spanish and English, which would give him an advantage in life. He was on a different path than the one I travelled on and was going to grow up to be a good person. He was Grandma's boy all right, and she treated him like her own. He called her Mama, and she deserved the respect.

I tried to tell them not to bother coming to see me during the frigid winter months, but they refused to listen. They reminded me that they were my parents and should be able to come whenever they wanted.

My family always stood by my side no matter what but seeing me locked up tore them up. My mother showed signs of stress, and I hated knowing I was the cause. I knew I had to continue working through *The Big Book*. No ifs and or butts about it!

As our visit was ending, they told me that a cousin had just been released from prison after serving a twenty-four-year sentence. *Wow, that was a long time to be behind bars.* I told them I would be home soon because I had served ninety percent of my short five-year sentence. We exchanged hugs, and I told them all that I loved them very much.

WORKING THE PROGRAM

Back at our pod, we were planning a big meal for Christmas. All the Hispanic inmates were planning to get together and eat like one big happy family. On Christmas Day, we had a big feast in the chow hall, and everyone got to take back what they couldn't finish to their pod.

It tore me up knowing I would miss seeing Justin open his gifts and playing with everyone. I prayed that this would be my last Christmas incarcerated.

Alcoholic's Anonymous - Working the Program

On New Year's Eve, it started to snow, and it looked beautiful outside. Most of us watched the bowl games. The one I thought was best was between Mississippi State and Texas A&M. The Bulldogs beat the Aggies in the snow in overtime 43-41. After the final game, we watched movies all night. Some watched the final count down from Times Square in New York City.

THE NEW YEAR

A new year and not knowing what lay ahead, I liked where I stood and the direction I was heading. I knew if I kept working on my program and maintaining my faith, everything would fall into place. I kept asking God what was best for me and that he would surround my loved ones with His Holy Angels.

I thought often about my family and wondered what little Justin was up to. Occasionally, I thought about Red, hoping and praying that God had touched her. Even though eleven months had passed since I told her to get lost and to stay out of my life, deep inside, I still loved and cared about her as a person and her kids. I thought about how they were doing and would pray God's best over them. That is the love of God and that no one can take that away. I thanked Him for everything and most of all for showing His love to us all.

January rolled by without much fanfare. I was attending meetings and taking a Life Skills class, which I had to complete before I could ever be released. My Electrical Class teacher was letting me attend his class the second part of the day. My agenda was packed, I had AA on Tuesday, N/A on Thursday, Church on Saturday, and Life Skills class weekday mornings from 6:50 to 10:00. My last day in Electrical Class was January 1, 2001.

I received a letter from my former neighbor Mike Gomez. My family knew he and his wife Ruth since moving to the Dallas area in 1986. They were great people, and we all enjoyed each other's company. I was so happy to hear from him. I wrote him a letter and told him how I was doing and when I thought I might be on my way home.

There were two guys leading our church services, Gary and Ruben. I always enjoyed the music because of the way they played. Gary was a famous person and played the keyboard while Ruben played the guitar. Their band was extraordinarily talented.

I spoke with the chaplain and asked if I could call home. He arranged the call, and Mother answered the phone. I was so happy to hear her voice. She told me everything was fine, and everyone missed me. I didn't get to chat with my little prince Justin because he was out eating pizza with one of my nephews named David. Strangely, my incarceration had brought my family closer together. God always brings good out of every situation.

Early in February, I was expecting a visit from family, but no one showed up. I didn't worry because I knew that my GOD protected and looked over my loved ones. I focused on my programs and continued to share whenever I could, which made me feel good about my life and the direction I was heading. I was preparing myself for the Free World.

On February 17, I was called out for a visit, which came as a surprise because. It was my father, Justin, my little sister, and her daughter Madison, who had grown so much since their last visit. Everyone was sitting together, and little Justin was not saying a word. I thought something might be wrong, but my sister told me he had eaten something that made him sick. They took him to the restroom where he was able to throw up. When he returned, he was all over me. Man, I loved my son so much and could not wait to get out and enjoy life with him.

My father looked good, we reflected on old times and chatted about everything. He told me that I had come a long way. I told him because of the direction I had taken in life I should have died long ago. We both knew I was telling the truth.

As February passed my meetings were getting very intense but interesting. We opened up and shared about ourselves in ways we had never done before. Those talks were like keys unlocking our recovery. I always knew that the more I participated the better I would feel about myself. Many of us were doing well, but we all knew the real temptations would be waiting for us out in the Free World. We talked about the fact that it is not about getting out but staying out. We talked about how to deal with temptations when they approached and warned each other that they would come in many ways. Unfortunately, the **recidivism rate in Texas was about 20%, so only a small percentage would be successful.**

March 3 was graduation day for the Vocational Classes and the G.E.D. participants. It had been raining all week, and I wondered if my family was going to be here. I knew the area and streets around the prison were flooded. We rehearsed on that Friday before the ceremony, so I knew what to do and was looking forward to the event. I kept thinking to myself that I hoped my family didn't come so they wouldn't get caught in the dangerous weather.

I worried about my family and my baby pie of the world little Justin. I understood if they missed my ceremony because I wanted them to be safe.

GOD IS REAL

Saturday 3, 2001 at 6:40 a.m., I was wide-awake and lying on my bunk bed waiting for guards to count everyone. Once they finished, I draped a sheet around the top part of the bunk so the light wouldn't wake up my cellmate. I performed my usual morning routine by taking a dump and shaving.

Justin Adam and me 2001

Limestone County Detention Center 2001

I always brushed my teeth in the shower, and before long I was all clean and back in my cell waiting for the second count to be completed. They wanted to make everyone was accounted for and where they should be. I could see that it was pouring outside. The guards started to call us out of the pods one at a time from the west end to the east end. We were excited, and they searched us as usual and told us to go to our classrooms.

Soon, we were lined up for graduation and a band started to play. We marched into the large room one class at a time. Suddenly, I saw my little sister, Alma, sitting on the front row waving at me, and then I saw the rest of my family. My wonderful mother was sitting next to my little Prince Justin, and next to him was my sister and her little boy, Jacob. I thought about how he had grown since I last saw him. Jacob had always been big from the beginning and reminded me of my older brother, Beto, when he was little.

I waved at my mother and my little Justin and told them I loved them. My love for them welled up inside of me and made my eyes water. I tried not to show emotion and thought to myself, *thank you, my Lord, for blessing me with this family that has supported me in every way.*

Our class was the first class, and I was the second student on the front row. A few people were asked to say a few words, and then we prayed before the ceremony got under way. Before long, graduation had ended, and we joined our families in the back of the gym to enjoy some doughnuts, cake, and cookies.

Then, we were told to return to our Pods for another count but that we would be allowed to see our families again. You should have seen my little boy; he could not wait for me to hold him. It was such a blessing getting to play with my little prince and my little nephew, Jacob.

Mother had taken Justin to have his eyes checked and he was given new glasses. He had them on and was getting used to them. Before, he would try to pull them off but now he was learning that he needed them to see. I was so proud of him.

Justin Adam and me 1999

The family told me that Red, David, and Ashley had come by to invite Justin to Natali's birthday party that was to be held the following week. She had just turned five years old. They wondered if I were going to object to him going, but I said it would be great. I had no problem with him going whatsoever.

In fact, I missed Natali because I had always been there for her and loved her very much. The last time I held her was September of 1996 when she was just eight months old. The last time I got to see her was in November at her grandmother's house before I left to be incarcerated.

We were wrapping up our visit, and I told my mother I had to return to my cell. I knew they were tired and needed to get something to eat. They left Dallas at 6:00 a.m. to be early to my graduation and not miss any of the day's events. We took some last pictures of all of us together. I got one of father, Justin, and me. Then the best picture was the one of just Justin and me, father and son. It was an amazing graduation celebration.

REVIVAL

After my family left, I headed toward the chow hall to get something to eat. There, I ran into the Chaplin. From deep inside, I thanked him for everything and for rescuing me from the destructive direction I had taken. He was leading church services late in the day because of the graduation and other activities that morning. Not too many inmates were in attendance, but the few that were there worshiped and praised our Mighty God.

In AA meetings I started noticing more people getting involved and sharing about their desire to change. Everyone needed a change in his life. Our time together was remarkably interesting and went by in a hurry when everyone shared. Their stories really hit home to me, and I would think *Wow, we are not that much different.*

The following week, about twenty college students came from Northwestern University. They were all young Christians and full of the Holy Spirit. These kids were on spring break, and instead of going on vacation or to the beach with their friends they chose to visit us. How beautiful!

Praying to God

We heard testimonies from a few of them, and some shared how they had been abused by their parents. Their stories brought tears to my eyes. God had enacted a change in their lives, their faith had increased. Out of their pain they found joy. We could see the love of God on their faces. Everything is possible with God. I was touched in such a way that our time together made my day.

The weekend of September 23 and 24 a revival service was held in Spanish and English, and several volunteers had come to host the event. I had been attending more Spanish services because they were different from before. They had grown larger in size, and inmates were giving up their old ways, longing for something different. So, I joined my Spanish brothers during the revival, but on the final day, both Spanish and English groups worshiped and praised God together. We sang "Let the River Flow" and "The River of God." It was an amazing time.

I decided to go up front for healing and to get prayer for my family. The volunteers were powerful prayer warriors. As I stood with my hands, in the air one of the ladies came to me and said,

"Just relax and let go." Suddenly, something enormously powerful came over me, and I started to fall backwards. I was able to fight it and stood strong, but I had no idea what had happened. It was a scary moment, but deep inside I knew God was with me.

I began thanking Him for rescuing and saving me. Once again, I asked Him to forgive all my wrongdoings and not to leave any of my loved ones behind. I also asked Him to keep an eye on my family, friends, Red and David, Ashely, Natali, Red's mother, and David's family. I ended my prayer asking for protection from any evil people around me, and I felt blessed.

BLESSINGS FROM ABOVE

Some people were saved from their sins that night and born again in the Spirit. Others experienced physical healing. One of the volunteers who asked for prayer walked up to the front on crutches. All I remember is that the crutches fell off to the side, and he walked back to his seat without them. He had been healed, what a night.

After witnessing his healing, I went to a man on the volunteer team and told him that I had a pain in my stomach. It had been bothering me lately, and I thought I had an ulcer. I asked him to pray and when he finished there was no more pain. Unbelievable!

GOD BLESS US ALL

Feeling good about myself and where I was in life, I thought about little Justin and the life ahead that was waiting for us. I saw myself going with him to the park, playing football and basketball games, and grocery shopping. Since my profession had always been in the retail industry, grocery shopping was one of my favorite past times. I intended to teach him right from wrong and be the best father I could be to him. I knew deep inside that our time together was going to be wonderful. I was eight months and twelve days from my release date.

There were many times in the past that I would cry inside, and just fuss about everything. But none of my old issues mattered anymore because of the joy that was inside of me. I still had to be careful because of the people around me. From past experience, I had learned not to trust anyone. Some people tried to trick you to get something for nothing. They would say they needed money because they were hungry or that they wanted to buy something for their family. Most of the time, I found out they were just lying and wanted money to gamble with. I used to let their behavior upset me.

Now, I understood that though God wants us to help the needy. He also warns us about people who put on fake masks to get their way. I also learned that we are to do what we can to help people, and if they try to pull a scam on us, it doesn't matter. He will bless us in return one way or the other, sometimes giving us three times what they took.

APRIL FOOL'S DAY

The month of March ended on a Saturday, and I went to church to give the Lord thanks for all His many blessings. I also had gotten some good news from my attorney about the motion we had filed to keep me in the States. The United States Supreme Court had ruled that a felony D.W.I. was not a Crime of Violence, which meant that it was not considered an aggravated felony that warranted deportation under U.S. immigration law. I would no longer be facing removal proceedings. Praise the Lord! I told others that they were in the same situation to get their cases re-opened. There was a big possibility they could get them dismissed.

I was still flying high from the revival service, and the next day was April Fool's Day. I reflected back to 1977 and what an amazing year it had been. Previously in the book I shared about my experience attending the Led Zeppelin concert. Now, twenty-four years later, I was daydreaming about the experience.

Led Zeppelin 1977

If you remember Robert Plant was having issues with his voice, so they decided to cancel the show. Everyone was devastated, but as luck would have it, they rescheduled it for a later date, April Fool's Day. Closing my eyes, I could hear the roar of the crowd when Zeppelin played their signature song, "Stairway to Heaven" and the sound of Jimmy Page's amazing guitar and John Bonhams drum solo. A concert to remember.

Led Zeppelin posters

Awakening from my daydream, I thought *I will attend many more concerts*. I stayed inside the dorm to avoid the heat. Whenever I went outside, I would sweat and have to wash my clothes. Instead, I wrote a letter to my mother and sister Mary letting them know the good news and included a card for my little Justin. I could see myself doing yard work around the house and him trying to help. The day ended with thoughts about the life that awaited us.

LET THE RIVER FLOW

As previously mentioned, I was mostly attending the Spanish services. I had been going more often and loved being there. Probably because they moved my spirit. I also felt like I had to be there for others who were walking the narrow road that I had traveled.

I received the paperwork from my attorney and was focused on getting it filled out quickly. I had someone helping me and told them not to wait too long.

That evening around 6 p.m., I was able to watch some Christmas videos. After the videos, some of us watched the women's basketball finals between *Purdue* and the *Notre Dame Fighting Irish*. The game came down to the wire and Notre Dame won by two points, 68 to 66, after trailing most of the game. On April 2nd we watched the Men's NCAA Basketball Championship between Duke and Arizona. Duke won by ten points defeating Arizona, 82 to 72.

April 5 was my birthday, and I turned thirty-nine years old. To me it was just another day, I didn't think about making a big deal about it. However, I did think that if I were in the Free World, I would treat myself to a big ole double meat cheeseburger.

The next day was a Friday, and there was a concert scheduled in our unit featuring our praise group. They played several songs, but the best song of the night was "Let the River Flow". That song made my spirit move. I found myself standing and praising the Lord, which I really enjoyed. The song was everyone's favorite, and we all sang along. I thought they should rename the song Let the Spirit Flow because the Holy Spirit really flowed through the room touching all who were in attendance. After church, I was hungry and asked my cellmate if he had eaten. He said no, so I made a decent spread for both of us, and we ate well.

LIFE IS A MINISTRY

I was looking forward to the next day, Saturday April 7, because my family was scheduled for a visit. At 8 in the morning an officer woke me up because I had overslept. I was caught off guard and a little surprised. As usual I did my business, brushed my teeth, shaved, and put on some aftershave. I was outside the door before count time, which was at 9:00 a.m.

My family always came between 11:30 and 1:00, so I expectedly waited to see who had come to see me. It was my mother, little sister Mary, little niece Madison, and of course Justin, my little troublemaker, and baby pie of the world. Mother was waving at me and as soon as I entered the room, Justin ran into my arms. I gave the rest of the family hugs, and we all sat down. Justin was talking nonstop, and I was amazed how much he had grown. Madison had started taking her first steps, which was beautiful to see.

Mother, Matthew, and Justin Adam *Justin's first day in school*

Disney World *The family at Disney World*

We talked about my plans when I got out and the new life that awaited me. I thought about all the things I had missed while Justin was growing up. I also knew that Justin was going to be a part of my future ministry of helping others not to take the fork in the road I had taken.

Thursday, April 12 I signed up to help the Mike Barber Ministries team that was setting up at our unit. Our Chaplin called me in for a short meeting, and he let all the volunteers know what needed to be done. I got to help set up the stage, lights, and chairs. The service was scheduled for 6:30 p.m., so I had just enough time to take a quick shower, get cleaned up, and be ready for the count.

Justin's classmates

Winter in Dallas, Texas

Justin Adam Camacho at six-years-old

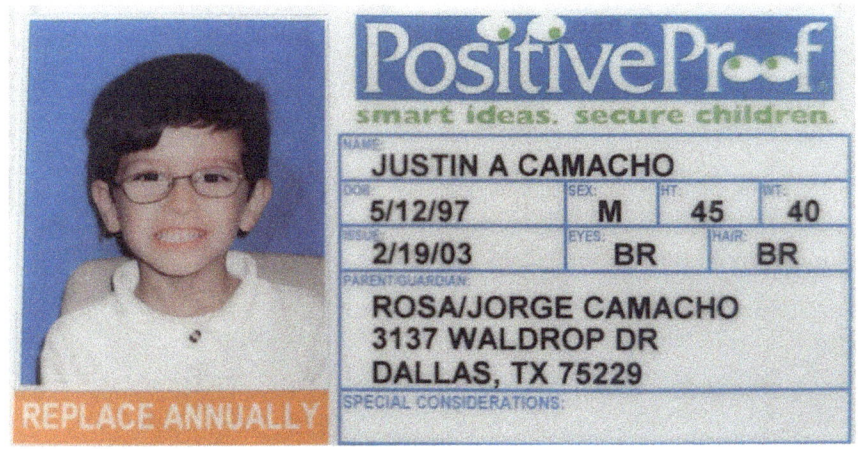

Justin's I.D. card 2003

Justin Adam and Natali May

The show did not start as planned because the guards had trouble clearing the count, but it wasn't long before Gary, who was with the ministry, started singing. But the main event was Isaac, who sure could preach. He shared the Good News with us and gave us a talk out of Genesis in the bible. We had a few more songs by Gary before the night was over, and I thought about what an excellent service it had been.

The next day, I was called back to The Chaplin's office. I thought he was going to ask me to help out with a service, but instead, he caught me off guard when he said I was invited to do an interview with Mr. Mike Barber.

When we met, Mike asked a few routine questions about my life. Then, he asked, "What were you doing before you turned to God? Tell us about the old you and the new you."

I told him, "I wasn't doing anything right. I was lying, drinking, and not living right. I was making my loved ones suffer for all my mistakes." Then, I told him everything God had done for me. I told him about my transition spiritually and how I had felt the presence of God. I said, "Everything I am going through was supposed to happen for the better because God had a plan for me."

In closing, he asked what advice I would give others. I said, "Everyone needs to repent, ask for forgiveness, and turn away from their evil ways. Let God work in their lives because everything is possible with God."

I was able to share with him how he had influenced my life and helped me to see the real me. I spoke about how touched I was by his testimony in 1997 when I was at Hutchin's State Jail. I let him know that was when I started to believe that God could work with anyone and change people's lives.

I remember his famous line, "What we think is destruction can be construction to God. That day he told us if we believed in God to look up to the sky. We all looked up and there were just clouds. He then said, "God just took a picture of you all. He will be there every step of the way. He can change things around if you will seek Him and give your Life to Christ."

After our interview, we had a prayer meeting with all the counselors and prayed for each other. We prayed for our families and everyone who came to mind. Before long, our beautiful session ended. It had been "bad to the bone," like Mr. Barber would always say.

Deep inside, I felt good about everything and was proud about where I stood with God. I had never felt like this ever. During my life, I got high many times, but nothing could replace the high I was feeling now; it was freedom.

All you have to do is ask God into your heart, and just like me you will begin changing little by little. That is the Lord's process.

DREAM ON

May 3 was the last day in my Life Skills Class. We had fun, and the guards let us watch a bunch of good movies. We dreamed on about the better days that lay ahead.

It was also the beginning of the first round of the of the N.B.A. play-offs. The Dallas Mavericks were down 2 to 1 in the best of five series against the Utah Jazz. The next game Dallas blew them out by almost thirty points and tied the series 2-2. On Thursday May 4, after trailing by as much as sixteen points for most of the game Dallas came back and pulled off an upset beating them 84 to 83. It was an exciting game, and all Dallas fans were cheering.

Saturday, May 5, I woke up, and all I could think about was that it was Justin's birthday. How I missed him and my family and wanted so badly to be with them. I went to church, and it was an exceptionally good service. Some people came and shared their testimonies about how they had changed from who they once were. I heard myself in each of their stories and could relate. I thought, *Heck, I should go up there and tell some of my story*. Well, around 3:15 p.m. the Chaplin gave me that opportunity.

Later I was able to call home, and my mother answered. She thought she was talking to my brother until I said, "Where is my troublemaker?" Immediately, she knew it was me. I was only six and a half months from going home. I wished I could explain to her everything about my incarceration, but there just wasn't time. I wanted her to know that God had allowed my incarceration, and now I felt His love inside of me. I knew she would understand and telling her was an opportunity that waited for me. I could see myself doing the positive things out in the Free World. I dreamed about the better days that lay ahead.

I continued my AA and N/A meetings where we always had good topics. I encouraged everyone to work on his program because if they distanced themselves from the program, they risk falling back into their old habits. I let them know that it might not happen right away, but eventually they would fall back into old habits. It happened to me too many times even though I knew better. We talked about getting out and staying sober. I told them, "It is not about getting out. It is about staying out and living a life without the use of alcohol or drugs. That will be the real test awaiting us all out in the Free World. We will be tempted in many ways. Some of us might not make it. Some will be too busy to stick with the program or make excuses to get out of attending. You will have to make room in your life for the program, or you will not be successful, and the way back to sobriety will be harder. You have to want it from within and take your sobriety seriously."

On May 19, Mother, my older sister Elsa, my little niece Alexis, and my little troublemaker Justin came to see me. Justin ran into my arms once again. I was so happy to see them all. We talked about everything, and the time flew by. As always, we exchanged hugs, and I told my mother and my sister to tell everyone hello. I kissed my little boy and walked out of the visitation room. Looking back, he waved and threw kisses at me. He was something else, and I dreamed about the things we were going to do upon my release.

Justin Adam and me 2002

TOO GOOD TO BE TRUE

The day after Memorial Day I received a letter from my mother. She told me that someone from the parole board notified her and said I would be getting out in June. I could hardly believe that getting out was a reality. I gave God all the thanks for what He had done for me. He had rescued me from destruction and constructed me into what He planned me to be all along. I was so surprised I could not sleep at all that night.

I started thinking about Justin and started to look at my life differently than ever before. I knew for a fact that Justin and my journey together would be incredible, and that the world would someday read all about it. Our journey would be the story of the Decade.

I called home to get the specifics about my release. She wasn't home but I spoke to my older sister. She told me I would be getting a visit from mother, and she would explain everything about the conversation with the person from the parole board and the case worker who had come to the house.

I did not know what to expect or what was going on, but I knew it would be a miracle to get out early. I thought *I could be writing the last chapter of my ups and downs in this place.* I could start to focus seriously on my new life in the Free World. I knew the road was narrow and was going to be exceedingly difficult because of the temptations of the world. I knew they would be real and waiting for me. I knew they would come in many forms.

No one said life was going to be easy; in fact, I learned that the road ahead would be bumpy. The true test would be coming. So, I started to think about all the lessons that I had learned to prepare myself for life on the outside. The primary objectives would be to stay focused on Christ and surround myself with good people. Inside, I questioned if I was ready.

I thought about the Apostle Peter walking on the water before Jesus. When he lost his focus and took his eyes off of Jesus fear set in and he started to sink. I knew I must keep my focus and eyes on Christ. I continued to ask God for strength and for His protection from the evil one. I thanked the Father Almighty for all He had done for me and my loved ones and how he had surrounded me with many righteous people.

On Saturday, June 30, 2001, my father, mother, and my little troublemaker Justin came to visit. They told me the person who had contacted them from the parole board had made a mistake. Evidently there were many conversations between the members of the parole board and the decision was made not to release me.

I would not be getting out early after all. After hearing the news, the thought occurred to me, *just trust God and let the journey unfold.* The Lord was allowing me to be tested spiritually, so I embraced the decision and set aside all the excitement about joining my family in the free world.

The Lord allows all of us to go through trials and tribulation so that we can search our hearts and make sure we are serious about changing. How does one really know unless they are faced with a tough and trying time?

As always it was a pleasure seeing my parents. Toward the end of our time together Justin told me he had another Daddy beside me. I knew it was my father and was grateful he had both of us in his life.

READY FOR THE FREE WORLD

Around the middle of August, Mother came back for a visit. As I entered the visitation room, I saw mother holding this little girl and I wondered if there was another child in our family, so I asked, "Who is the little girl." She said, "It's Madison."

"Wow," was all I could say, for she had grown so much I hadn't recognized her. Also joining her for the visit was my nephew Matthew, and my little prince and troublemaker, Jusin.

I still felt weighed down seeing how my incarceration affected my family and all the trouble I was putting them through. I cried on the inside knowing if I had been more responsible, I would not be in this situation, and they would not have to travel all the time to visit. At least there was an end in sight, I knew deep inside that I would be returning home soon and when that day came, I would be thanking God for all that He allowed to happen.

As mentioned previously, I should have died several times when I was messing around with dope, weed, and alcohol. But knowing He had a plan for my life, God spared me. Placing my trust in Him allowed me to be molded into a better person. I needed to get everything right with God first before I could let go of the bitterness and pain. Now, I was no longer ashamed of my past because I knew where I was going and what I was going to do for Him. My Father Almighty would always be there by my side.

Every morning, I thanked Him for giving me one more day. It was August 28, and I was down to my last one hundred days. God willing, I would be going home soon. My flesh doubted *Will you be successful in the Free World, or will you be one of the poor souls that returns to his old ways?*

I learned many things during my time, but one of the most important was to rebuke the negative thoughts. I planned to use every tool that I had acquired to thrive on the outside and never return to these walls. I had seen a lot of people come and go over the past few months and decided I was just going to relax and take it one day at a time. I was ready!

AA taught us to let go, let God, to take it easy, and to live one day at a time. I had learned to be open, honest, and patient. I'm not saying that the AA works automatically for everyone. The desire has to come from within. Each person has to make a serious decision by asking himself, "Do I have a problem? Do I want to be sober?" Depending on their answers, AA is a powerful tool. But everyone must do the work individually and stay in the program for it to be a success.

The last week of August seemed to fly by. One of the pods was locked down because a few people had become infected with the chickenpox virus. The weather was cold and rainy, and I caught myself daydreaming about life on the outside. I thought about Red and our times together. I knew she was living with someone, and it didn't bother me one bit. I also knew she would do her best to cast her spell on me in hopes of getting me back. No! No! No! I wanted to talk to her about how my life was different and make sure she knew that our time together had ended, and we were going separate ways. I was prepared to move on with my life.

9/11/2001

Tuesday September 11, 2001, I went to work early around 6:30 because I knew there was a lot that needed to be done. We all completed our work and were released earlier than usual at about 8:20. I stuck around to make some cheeseburgers, and as I was finishing people were talking about some kind of attack on the U.S.

Twin Towers in New York City

Twin Towers attacked on 9/11/ 2001

I left to see what was happening. The news reports said that the World Trade Center had been hit by two hijacked planes and both towers had collapsed. They said another plane had crashed into the Pentagon while another crashed into an open field. We were under a major terrorist attack, and the U.S. closed all borders and ceased all flights.

THE UPS AND DOWNS OF J.C.

Second plane heading towards the towers

Twin towers billowing smoke

I cried out to my Lord and asked Him to comfort the families who were impacted. I started to think about the prophetic signs spoken about in the bible. *When will the end come?* The bible gives the answer in Matthew 24:36, "But about that day or hour no one knows, not even the angels in heaven, nor the Son, but only the Father."

But Jesus did say that there would be certain signs we should be watching for, the signs of the times. I thought about verses 6 and 7 in Matthew 24, "You will hear of wars and rumors of wars, but see to it that you are not alarmed. Such things must happen, but the end is still to come. Nation will rise against nation, and kingdom against kingdom. There will be famines and earthquakes in various places."

The events were the beginning of sorrows, and all we could do was pray for the victims and their loved ones. President George W. Bush told the American people that the persons responsible would be hunted down held responsible. That the American people would seek Justice.

Thousands of innocent people had been killed; no one knew for sure how many. For days after the attack, volunteers searched for missing people. Dead bodies were everywhere, and the nation feared some people might never be found.

News sources announced that Bin Laden, an Islamist militant leader and founder of a terrorist organization called al-Qaeda was behind all the attacks. The U.S. learned that the Afghanistan government had provided Bin Laden and his followers a safe haven. Along with our Allies we responded to the attack by bombing training bases throughout Afghanistan. Our government informed the Afghans that the bombing would continue until they either turned over Bin Laden or we captured him and brought him to the United States to stand trial.

Here at home, letters were being sent with traces of Anthrax to Postal Offices around New York City and to people in high places including the White House. It was crazy, four postal workers died and sixteen more were infected. A lot of people were in fear. No one knew what to expect or what might happen next.

The men in our unit prayed for peace throughout the world asking God to help the needy and to help those who had done wrong to repent.

Justin Adam and me 2001

THE WALLS UNIT AGAIN?

In the ensuing days I coped by executing my normal routine of going to meetings and church. I continued to replace all the negative thoughts with the positive and as the month of October was ending, I thought about Justin. Halloween was approaching and I envisioned him going trick or treating. I thought how much fun it would be holding his hand, being there for him, and letting him know his Daddy loved him. I constantly thanked my Father in heaven for holding my hand, comforting me, giving me peace of mind, and loving me like I had never felt before.

Thirty days and counting until I was set to be released. Needless to say, I was excited and couldn't wait to be out with my family and my little Baby Pie of The World. However, I kept my focus remembering never to forget how God had opened my eyes and touched my Heart. I cried out to Him and thanked Him once again for His many Blessings and for always being there for me. He loves each one of us. We are his precious pearls.

At the Walls Unit 2001

December 4, I was inventoried and ready to catch the chain the following day. Another person and I were sent to the Walls Unit in Huntsville, Texas. We arrived about 8:00 in the morning. Like I said earlier in the book, usually you were only sent to the Walls unit if you had a medical condition or were close to being released.

After settling in, we headed to the chow hall, but in route were suddenly stopped and told to wait. I was close to the front of the line and saw that a fight had broken out between two inmates. One was a heavyset person and the other a tall, thin fellow who was swift and quick. The thin person was beating the heavier one until the guards stepped in and stopped the fight.

During my five-year period of incarceration, I witnessed many fights. It seemed the fights were always over some kind of neighborhood/homeboy rivalry.

That would be my final meal and my last day at the Walls Unit; my prison days were coming to an end.

CONVICTIONS

Unfortunately, it was not my last day to be held in custody. Instead of being released to go home the I.N.S. transported me to a detention center in Houston, Texas. The facility was ridiculously small, something I was not accustomed to.

Once I figured out what was happening, I called home, and my sister Mary answered. I told her I.N.S. had reopened the old case against me. They were saying I still had a conviction from when I lived in California. In 1997, it had been determined that someone else had stolen my identity and claimed to be me. So, what they were saying now didn't make any sense whatsoever.

I asked for some extra money in case they held me longer than expected. I also asked her to look up all my convictions between 1980 to 1996. I wanted to compare them and see if any matched the case they were bringing against me.

I reflected on the advice I had received from my attorney about my last conviction. He told me if I wanted to get rid of my ten-year probation, I needed to plead guilty to the new D.W.I. and weed possession. I would receive no more than a two-year sentence, but my probation would be wiped away for good. Of course, the judge sentenced me to five years.

My sister told me that the charge was not on my record, so I started wondering if the person who had been using my identity had anything to do with the renewed investigation.

It was Sunday December 9 and since all I could do was wait, I watched my cowboys win their fourth game of the year against the New York Giants. Unlike my situation, it appeared they were heading in a good direction and were destined to be good again soon. People had been laughing at them, but it wouldn't be long before those same people would be rooting for them again.

COURT IN HOUSTON

On Friday December 14, 2001, I called home, and my sister Alma answered. She told me that my I.N.S. court date had been moved to the following Monday. I talked to my family about the strategy my attorney wanted to use. She planned to get me released and have my case moved to Dallas. I felt confident knowing God would be watching over me, because with God everything is possible.

Before ending our call, Alma was blunt with me saying, "Jorge, if you ever mess up again, the family will not help you anymore." I assured her that I had made up my mind long ago about living a different life. There would be no more drinking and drugging. I told her the Father Almighty had taken away my urge to drink and use. I told her that my actions would speak louder than words, that I was going to show the family I was serious and gain back their trust and respect.

All I wanted was to move on with my life and spend time with my little Justin. I felt frustrated with where I was. I was used to my routine of going to meetings, church, and doing recreational activities. Now everything had come to a stop.

I just had to wait and try to get used to being there. I read my Bible and continued to ask God to help me with this temporary situation and to grant me patience. Many times, before He worked on my behalf even putting special people in my path.

I was watching television one day and thinking about my current situation and what I was planning to do. In the same room was a Christian brother, Bob talking about the precious gifts God had in store for us, but in order to receive them, we had to do His will not ours. I could tell he had the Spirit of God in him because the way he talked and put scriptures together made sense. He said some things that touched my heart and really opened my eyes.

Lately I had thoughts that my family was to blame for my situation, which was foolish. Listening to Bob rebooted my mind, and I was reminded how wonderful my family was and how blessed I was to have them by my side from the very start. I was re-energized to get things done, and when I attended church, I felt much better. It became obvious to me that God still had things He wanted me to learn.

Monday December 17, I went to court where I was able to talk to my attorney and go over the paperwork and discuss our plan. She was one of the best female lawyers in Dallas. I could see my mother and father in the background; they looked stressed out. My little sister, Mary, was there with my little troublemaker Justin and my niece to show their support. I had no idea where they got the money to pay the attorney, but they were determined to get me out of the facility as soon as possible. I never wanted them to see them look like that ever again, especially my mother.

The court proceeding went smoother than any of us expected. The judge was in a good mood and issued a $2,000 bond, which we were able to post. This would allow us to fight the case from the outside in the free world. For the first time, I knew for sure I was on my way out. I thought about freedom and the new life that awaited me. I thanked the Lord because He had made my release possible. Many people talk about their luck, but to me there is no such thing as luck, only God who is in charge. Soon I would be catching His chain and heading back to Dallas.

I called Alma and told her the good news about the bond. I let her know that we would get the money back once everything was finalized. I told her the attorney was using the fact that father was born in Texas and had the ten-year necessary requirements for me to obtain my citizenship.

A few days later I was talking to some of my friends about what we needed for our cells and making out a commissary list. An officer appeared and told me that the list was not going to be necessary. I was on the way out! I was going to be with my family for Christmas and get to hold my little Prince Justin, my baby pie of the world!

While waiting for the paperwork to be processed, a small group of believers met in the dayroom. I prayed aloud, "God, may you continue to bless the ones that are loyal to You. Thank you for the many rewards You provide for those who obey Your word and do righteous things, AMEN."

THE UPS AND DOWNS OF J.C.

Amen to God our Father

FREE AT LAST

I started to get nervous, and then it finally hit me: I was going home. It was December 2001, and I was homeward bound. I waved to my friends and walked out the doors of the detention center.

My sister drove to the side of the building where everyone got out and we hugged. I hugged my mother, my wonderful father, my little sister Mary, and of course my little troublemaker Justin. He sat beside me all the way home. My mother was very emotional and broke down crying. Her tears had been building up all those years.

City of Dallas 2001

Dallas skyline

Margaret McDermott bridge in Dallas

Reunion Tower 2001

Free at last in 2001

The Pegasus of Dallas

I was free at last and about four hours away from Dallas. At the time, my family was living on the west side of Love Field Airport. As we got closer to Dallas, I could see that beautiful city. When we arrived at the house, the rest of my family was waiting and together we all celebrated my freedom.

City of Dallas at night

I knew that I would need to adapt to my newfound freedom in the days and weeks ahead. Justin wanted to be with me all the time and even slept in my bed. He couldn't get enough of being with me after all the time we had been apart. I was so happy to finally be there for him.

I prayed every night asking my God to continue to give me the strength to be successful. I knew it was just a matter of time before I would run into some of my old friends and would need to distance myself from them.

TEMPTATION AND BEGINNING LIFE IN THE FREE WORLD

Some family members and friends who came to see me would drink in front of me. I knew that I would be tested repeatedly. But fortunately their drinking had no effect on me; I had lost all desire for alcohol.

On Christmas Eve, I went over to one of my aunt's houses for a big dinner Mexican feast. There was incredible Mexican tamales and all of my favorite dishes. There was also plenty of liquor, beer, and wine. One of my cousins asked me to pop the cork on a bottle of wine. Instead of being rude and saying no, I said, "Sure bring it over." I opened it and some of the wine got on my hand, which I casually washed off. I then went outside and stood by the big bonfire that one of my family members had lit.

That was just the first time I was tested, but similar events were to happen over and over. Each time I just thought to myself, *No thanks.* Usually, I would go watch television alone or find something else to do and reflect on what I learned in the AA program, "Change people, places, and things."

Of course, I was never going to walk out on my family because they helped me in so many ways. They were not the problem; I had been the problem all along. They knew I couldn't drink, but they were able to drink responsibly and function normally, something I was not capable of doing.

On Christmas Day, my mother made a big turkey along with many other goodies. Family members brought ham and other items that were requested. My little sister's husband, Whitney, made his famous green bean casserole, an excellent dish. My little sister was blessed to have a man in her life who did so much for her and took exceptionally loving care of their beautiful children.

All the children enjoyed opening their gifts. I stood there and watched while my little troublemaker Justin opened his. It blessed me to see how happy he was and the joy on his face. Occasionally he would look over at me and smile. I was so happy for him.

On New Year's Eve I went to my brother Beto's house. He had just bought a big brick home for his family. He had a wonderful wife, and she was an excellent cook. She made a kind of Spanish stew that was incredible.

There was a lot of liquor, wine, and beer being served and I asked myself, *can you be around this environment without triggering a relapse?* Initially I thought it would be risky and dangerous. That all the work I had put into bettering myself could go right out the window or down the drain. But I was not influenced or bothered by their drinking.

God had taken the desire to use out of my life. I knew the potential was always in front of me, but there was no way I was going to relapse. I had one person that mattered to me more than anyone, Justin, and I was not going to let him down.

That night Justin and I watched a part of the movie Babe before he fell asleep. After putting him to bed, I changed the channel and watched the countdown at Times Square where everyone was celebrating the New Year in New York City. Then I stepped outside and listened to the fireworks and heard some people shooting guns. I thought about shooting mine but given my situation decided it would not be wise.

On New Year's Day, my little brother and his girlfriend made black-eye peas, corn bread, and some other goodies. I got myself a bowl of black-eye peas and some corn bread. I headed for the living room, where I settled in and watched all the bowl games. I said a little prayer asking God to continue looking over me and most of all to help me in all situations. Knowing He knew what He had in store for me, I gave Him thanks for everything.

STORE #3585

BEST IN CLASS

Having worked for Tom Thumb my whole career, I was well aware of how people needed to be treated. I was fortunate to work many hours at various locations and had some great store managers.

I was able to return to Tom Thumb as a produce clerk at the small Store #2544. From that point on, I never looked back. Eventually I would be asked to help set up other stores and get them ready for business. I earned my certification and became an Assistant Produce Manager and was awarded *Best in Class*.

Two years had passed since I got out of prison, and so far, life had been a success. God had blessed me with the people at the store and they allowed me to work many hours.

Before long I was promoted to Assistant Produce Manager for store #3585 located at John West and South Buckner Road on the east side of White Rock Lake.

Tom Thumb Store #3585

This would be the next step before getting an opportunity to be the Produce Manager and run the whole department. I planned to use the time efficiently to get a feel for everything so I would be prepared.

When I got to the store, the produce department had many issues. They were using watermelon bins as tables to hold products and the shelves were dirty. No one was making any effort; they had abandoned the department completely. It was awful.

On my first day I overheard someone telling Mr. Taylor, the Meat Department Manager, that all the produce equipment had been stored upstairs and was just sitting there because no one had the time to put it together. That made no sense to me. Mr. Taylor came up to me and introduced himself. He told me that the person running the produce department did not care at all about the store. He said customers were always complaining about certain items not being available. He would just tell them that the warehouse was out instead of reordering items. He was costing the store sales.

Mr. Mix was my first Store Director in 1986, but now was a District Manager. He was a great person who cared very much for everyone. He was all about customer service and had heard the complaints about the produce department. Knowing it was a total mess; he was looking for someone to take over the department at store #3585.

Mr. Mix and the store Director, Mr. Calvert, approached me one day and asked if I would like to take over the department. I responded expediently that I would, and they told me to go for it. The district office had heard good things about me and been told that I always found a way to get the job done. It appeared that everyone wanted my services because I was a go-getter. I was perceived as one of the most motivated individuals in the district. Thus, the reason for my promotion.

Cut fruit section

My produce department

The district's Produce Merchandiser, Pete Amaya, called and said he would be there the next week to help me start putting the department in order. He said all the equipment and the table parts were upstairs. I dug in and worked 30 hours straight from one day to the next. I was determined to put the department back in order and get the job done; my reputation was on the line. With the help of my Assistant Produce Manager, Cleone we were able to put most of the department back together.

The Produce Merchandiser came the following week as promised and brought along more table parts. When he saw the department his jaw dropped, he could not believe what had been accomplished. Needless to say, he was incredibly surprised and asked the Store Director who had done all of the work. The Director said, "Mr. Camacho did most of the work." Of course, I couldn't have accomplished anything without Cleone's assistance.

THE CORPORATE LIFE

Bringing the Produce Department back to life only took about six months. On August 8, 2003, the corporate office promoted me to the higher volume store #2566 located close to my home at the corner of Skillman and Abrams Road.

Tom Thumb pride

They had been compensated well but along with the promotion they rewarded me with a higher salary for my accomplishments.

The challenges at this store were not as bad, but the department needed work. It was rough around the edges and needed to be polished here and there. Being located near the Corporate Office, all the executive big wheels were constantly coming in and out of the store. This made my job even more challenging because everything had to look its best every day.

I had inherited a weak crew and knew I would need to rebuild from the ground up to make the necessary changes and be successful. There were two employees working for me, and I told them they needed to improve, or I would hire someone else. I also needed to find an Assistant Produce Manager who was strong and aggressive.

Me at the Corprate Office

Produce display

District team at the Tom Thumb food drive

Wanting to promote from within I noticed this one young man name Adan who had potential, he was the most motivated person on the store staff. He was one of a kind, the type of person who was hard to find. I had not seen his style being displayed in quite a while. I started collaborating with him and we came to an agreement. He was excited to be promoted to be my assistant.

PLAIN CRAZY

I stayed busy and started having fun working at this store. I still had to pick up my paycheck from my old location because the move came suddenly, and they hadn't transferred my paperwork.

I'm not mentioning any names out of respect, but I started dating this person from my old store. She was crazy about me and was trying to rush me into a relationship; things were moving too fast. She started talking about things you don't talk about until you have been together a few years. She told me she wanted to be a wife. I was shocked and surprised; I had known this person for only a couple of months. She started telling everyone I was her boyfriend. I told her to please slow down. One day, she called and asked me to help her out with money so she could fix her car. I knew she needed a brake job, so I gave her some money.

I finally got tired of her nonsense. She was very controlling, and I just wanted out. She would call and ask why I had not been calling her. I would tell her that I was extremely busy. Finally, I told her I just wanted to be friends and nothing else. Little by little, I distanced myself from her, and she got the message. I just wanted to be single.

ANOTHER CUTE ONE

The paperwork was finally transferred to my new location and I no longer had to go to the old location to pick up my paycheck. We had a cute office manager, and I used to flirt with her, but she was married. One day, I passed by the office and noticed another person working there. I had seen her before and thought to myself, *what a beautiful person.* However, I thought she was too young for me. She looked like she was around eighteen to twenty years old.

One day, I tried talking to her, but she was in a bad mood. A few days later, I went to pick up my check, and she was in the office. I was in line behind a few people staring at her. She looked up, and we made eye contact for about four seconds. When I finally got to the counter, we talked for a bit, and I introduced myself. Other people were behind me so I cut our conversation short so she wouldn't get in trouble.

Every now and then, I would go by to say hello and flirt with her. I asked if she was single. She told me she had a boyfriend, and I told her that I was interested.

One day, I called the store to check on my crew in the department and she answered the phone, I quickly asked to speak with my Assistant Produce Manager. Before transferring me, she asked how I had been doing.

I could always feel something when a female was showing an interest in me. My heart was telling me she was interested. I thought, *maybe she is not happy with her boyfriend.* Being drawn to her I asked if she would like to go out on a date. She said, "No."

I dropped by to see her and told her that since she was a single parent, like me, we could take the kids out to Chuck E. Cheese and while the kids had some fun, we could get to know each other a little better. She gave me her phone number and told me to call her after six o'clock that same day. When I called, her mother answered the phone and wanted to know who I was and how I knew her daughter. I told her it was a long story, and it sounded like she was laughing.

As it turned out, her daughter had never made it home, so me and my little troublemaker Justin and I decided to go somewhere by ourselves. I had been looking forward to going out with her knowing she had a cute little girl who was just a year older than Justin.

Even though she didn't appear to be interested I thought to myself, *could this be the one?* A perfect fit; a boy and a girl. The only other thing we would need is a small dog.

A few days later, I saw her, and she told me the reason she wasn't home was because she had been working late that night.

But then she said, "We could hang out some other time if you want." Knowing I liked her, I figured she had just been feeling me out to see how I would react. Some women are like that. However, we were not able to agree on another time.

I stopped by to see her from time to time and would tell her that I was crazy about her and that I was going to take her away from her boyfriend. Showing her, I was interested was a mistake on my part and as the weeks went by, I thought about giving up on her.

LUNCH-TIME

Something inside told me not to give up on her, so I asked her out one more time for lunch. To my surprise she said, "Okay." We walked over to Burger King across from the store and while we were eating, I told her how much I liked her. She just laughed and looked the other way before responding, "George, we are just going to be good friends. I'm too young for you. I'm only twenty-six."

I told her, "Well I'm only thirty-nine."

She said, "If you were 30 years old, then I wouldn't mind going out with you."

I realized the age difference was the reason she had acted cold toward me. I told her that age did not matter as long as there was honest communication and trust between two people. She seemed open to my counsel so I added, "As long as we were on the same page, the rest will fall into place overtime."

She joined me for lunch again and I asked for her address. I told her I wanted to send her something for Valentine's which was a few days away. She said I did not have to give her anything but gave me her address anyway. I did plan to get her something, but I was really just testing her to see if she would actually give it to me.

Over my lifetime I learned that when a person refused to give you their phone number or address it usually meant they were not interested. So, I kept thinking that she was leaving the door open for a relationship with me. For Valentines, I bought her a box of chocolates, a necklace, and some earrings. The next time I saw her

I told her that I had something for her, and she said I was crazy. I told her that I was crazy about her!

OKAY!

I went to my car, got the gifts, bought some roses in a small vase, and took them to her. I asked her to open them right away. A customer was looking on and rolled his eyes as if to say, "Romance at the office."

She opened them and her face went blank. I knew what she was thinking. I had done my part. Now, it was up to her to do hers. Of course, she still had this so-called boyfriend, but she did not seem to care much about him. She called me at work early one day, and when I picked up the phone, she told me she wanted to pick me up and buy me lunch. I said, "Okay, but what about your boyfriend?"

She paused for a second and then said, "We don't have a very good relationship."

I told her the reason I had come in early was because I planned to see a movie on my lunch break. She told me she would meet me at the AMC theater. Well, that never happened. She stood me up once again, something about her shadow of a boyfriend was not working and she had to head back to her place.

I thought, *this isn't working*. About the time I was ready to give up on her, she called and said she wanted to go out. We met up, grabbed something to eat, and just talked. After a while, we ended up at my house. She started sneaking around her boyfriend's back more to go out with me. From that time on we would either go to my place or occasionally a motel. She shared with me all the issues about her boyfriend and all her family problems.

She told me that if she ever broke up with her boyfriend, she would never date anyone else, but we could still go out as friends. Which meant friends with benefits.

One day it was raining cats and dogs, and I hadn't left the store all day. Around 7:00 p.m., I called to see if she wanted to join me for a bite to eat. She said maybe and then changed her mind, so I asked if I could drop by and just say hello. She said, "Sure."

I picked her up, and we went to Chili's. We talked about a lot of interesting things. She said something confusing, "My boyfriend is going to catch us someday and he better not ever try to hit me." I thought, *you need to leave the guy and spend more time with your daughter.*

Not wanting to stand in her way and having second thoughts I felt it was best to distance myself a little and let her decide what she really wanted. Knowing I could be with her anytime I decided we could always be friends, and who knew, one day things might change.

Our relationship had been off and on anyway and being the workaholic that I am, as time went by the only time we spent together was with our kids. Justin really liked her, and I actually thought I loved her. After sharing my thoughts with her she told me that our relationship might be heading in the right direction.

Soon after our talk I learned that she had caught the chain so to speak. She had broken up with her boyfriend and started dating another guy. Wow, deep inside I always knew she couldn't be trusted...

She came to visit me a few times, but there was no commitment. I just wanted to distance myself from her. I felt guilty knowing our relationship had been wrong. Finally, she decided to get married to one of her so-called boyfriends and settle down. I was happy for her, but that was the end for us.

I never messed around with a married person even though a lot of them would test me to see how far they could get. Learned that I didn't need to mess around with a women who was dating another man either.

Sometimes it was just PLAIN CRAZY.

OLD JERRY

In 2005 my District Manager asked if I would be open to working at Store #1925 located in Rowlett, Texas just east of Dallas, which was a higher volume store. At first it appeared that I was not going to be the Produce Manager, but since the position came with more responsibility the company offered me more money to make the move.

Jerry was the Store Director, and I asked his permission to speak with the Produce Manager about some ideas on how we could improve the department. He said, "We no longer have a Produce Manager, but a new person is starting tomorrow."

The next day, he came up to me and said, "George the new guy just arrived." As I looked around, he pointed at me and laughed.

As a Store Director, Jerry was different than anyone else in our district or any other district for that matter. He would take all the department managers out bowling or to eat at a fancy restaurant and pay for everything with his own money. He wanted us to simply get away from the store for a while.

NEVER BE LATE

At first, I did not want to go to the Rowlett location because it was far away, and my little Justin was still young. Jerry knew I would worry about him so he made sure I got off early during the week, so I could pick him up from school.

One time I was late because I got stuck in traffic on the way to his school. When I arrived, his teacher was there waiting for me. I had failed my son and felt unbelievably bad.

When we got in the car, he told me something that I will never forget, something that hit me really hard. He said, "I thought something had happened to you and wondered who was going to take care of me."

Hurting, I responded, "Nothing is going to happen to me."

But he was right, in a way, so I assured him that if anything were to happen that mother, Mary, and our entire family would be there for him, that he had a beautiful family who would be on his side, and they loved him very much. They would go way beyond what was necessary to make sure he was taken care of.

From that time on, I asked my mother if she could be more involved. She was so wonderful for helping me. I would call her if I got stuck at work or if on the way to get him from school, If I ever ran into traffic.

I vowed that I would never be late again, period. He was the Love of my Life, and I wanted everything for him.

BOSS AND FRIEND

Jerry came up to me one day and said, "Go to Dallas, pick up your son from school, and have him join us for lunch." He knew Justin and liked him. He also knew that being a single parent and raising a child was hard. Being a family man himself and loving his children, he related to my situation.

After working at the store for quite some time Jerry called me to his office saying he had some shocking news for me. I thought I had done something wrong. When I walked in, he smiled and said, "Today is a momentous day for you and a sad day for me. You are going back to Dallas because you have accomplished all your goals here and have done an outstanding job. The District Manager has an assignment that no one can manage but you. How would you like to take over the department at store #3522 located at Preston and Royal?

I didn't miss a beat saying, "I'd love to."

"You will be missed George."

OPPORTUNITIES

At work I remained positive and worked hard and as a result another opportunity would soon come knocking on my door. For the previous five years I had been working at Store #3522 located on Preston Road and Royal Lane. It was a great store, and I had gotten used to the area and all the customers. First Lady Laura Bush shopped there with her housekeeper. Let me tell you the Secret Service made sure no one got close to her. They were everywhere, one outside, one in the front of the store on his phone, and another nearby just in case. She was an extremely outgoing human being who was down to earth and who talked and greeted you just like you were one of her friends.

Simon & David store #2533

I remember my District Manager, Mr. Brian Bausch, telling me that there was an opportunity coming up soon, and he wanted me to take advantage of it. He told me there was going to be a new store opening at University Park and Inwood Road. He added that there were five Produce Managers fighting to get the position.

Mr.Brian Bausch, District Manager

He told me that I would be perfect for the job, and he handpicked me. I told him, "No thanks." I thanked him for the offer and the opportunity, but said I was happy where I was. He came again in two weeks and offered me the same store again. I told him I was close to home, and I was happy at my present location. He asked me why I would decline such a great offer.

He had the same attitude toward me that I had toward the cowboys. He cared about me and wanted me to be successful. He was always pushing to make me better and stronger overall.

He was a great individual who cared about everyone and went beyond to make sure you were successful and happy with the company. He had done so much for me in the past, and I was not about to let him down. He was hard but fair, and I always admired that kind of person.

I finally told Mr. Bausch what a great friend and boss he was and that I admired him for the things he did. I knew he needed to have his team on paper and ready to go when the store opened so I told him, "Do what is best for the company. If you feel I belong there so let it be."

He shook my hand and told the Store Director to give me ten days off. I was on my way to the new store after a short vacation.

Tom Thumb store #2990

Well, the first six to eight weeks were an amazing time at store #2990. We would sit at this long and wide table and strategize about what needed to be done. This was part of our normal daily routine. The meeting lasted quite a while so some of us would go execute then come back later to continue the discussion.

I remember setting up the nut table. It was the first table in the Produce Department that we could set up because the store was still under construction, and we were a long way from being ready to open. We were having fun and our time was relaxing. There was no pressure of any kind. The pressure would start the closer we got to opening day. But in the meantime, we enjoyed ourselves.

MR. CLARK

Our store director, Mr. Clark, was young and fun to work for. He sometimes got upset at all of us, but soon he would get back to normal. I don't remember the exact date we opened the store, but it was in November of 2010. That I remember because the following year the Dallas Mavericks were in the play-offs and won it all. I put up a banner I had been given from a vendor that worked for the Budweiser Company that said DALLAS MAVERICKS N.B.A CHAMPIONS.

The produce department

The organic section

When we opened the store, the sales were unbelievable. Our sales for the entire store just kept climbing, and we were doing great in the Produce Department. All those sales sure kept me busy. Opening that store was something I will always be proud of.

Wet-rack organic section at Tom Thumb #2990

The produce department

Our department was number one in sales in our district. I was even beating one of the top stores in the district that had a bigger department and more holding power than ours. Their produce manager came over and asked if he could look around. He came to the back room and asked me where all of my product was. I told him most of our products were truck to the shelf, except for the fast-moving and sale items. He was extremely impressed with my ordering process.

JORGE A. CAMACHO

**GEORGE CAMACHO
PRODUCE MANAGER**

The conventional wet-rack

I even had produce managers come from other stores and districts to learn what we were doing to be so successful. They all wanted to get ideas, so they could better compete with the stores in their own districts.

In 2012, our store director started becoming frustrated with many things. He would come in on his day off and get upset about the condition of the store. The produce department was standing tall and looking good, but he still criticized us. He came back over to me and apologized saying it had not been my department, but a department on the other side of the store. He told me that if he didn't get upset with as well everyone else, he could be accused of discrimination. Thankfully, he was transferred to a different store.

Jamie's wall - best in class

finest cut fruit section

MR. LANE

Mr. Scott Lane was my second Store Director at location #2990. He was a veteran in the retail industry as well as the armed forces. He would come around to review our departments and point out items that had been overlooked from the previous night, but he was very professional.

Mr. Scott Lane Store Director

He was a unique and outgoing and always thanked us for everything we did to help the store. He liked to say, "We couldn't do it without you." He also went out of his way to help customers. They didn't grow his kind on a tree, he was a rare find. The two of us got along simply great. In my opinion He is the Best Store Director, I have ever worked for…

There were many changes taking place within Tom Thumb overall while Mr. Lane was there. Corporate had discontinuing many popular items, like Peter Pan Peanut Butter during the resets. Customers were upset and thought the store director was to blame. Mr. Lane would try to explain, but many did not want to hear what he had to say. The store was located in a fancy area of Dallas close to Highland Park, and the people that lived there did not care what he told them, they just wanted the items and didn't mind paying extra.

He took a couple of weeks off and unknown to Tom Thumb he was being recruited by Kroger, one of our biggest competitors. Unfortunately, he ended up leaving after just four years' operating the store.

For the next six weeks, Mr. Bausch searched for the right person to be our third Store Director and finally made the decision to give Mr. Thorson the opportunity. He was operating a store #2503 down the street. I knew him well and had helped him out on many occasions.

At first everything seemed all right then suddenly he changed his attitude. He started putting unnecessary pressure on me. It got so bad at one point I thought he was trying to get rid of me or push me out. I told him that if he was not happy with me or my performance to transfer me to another store.

One morning I went to the office to do some paperwork and there was an email open on the computer. I saw it by accident, evidently someone had left the email open or forgot to close it. It was supposed to be my half day off, so I was trying to complete the work so I could leave for the day. The email said he wanted permission or approval to write up a department manager.

He was referring to me. So, I approached him and told him that if he did not want me at the store to just let me know that there were other stores that would take me in a heartbeat.

Other store directors used to tell me all the time that if things did not work out at my store to come to their store. Mr. Thorson said I was taking it the wrong way and that he wanted me there. However, word travels fast, and there was a rumor going around the store that he did not like me, and had plans to replace me with Joe, the produce manager from his previous store.

TWO WEEKS NOTICE

I knew he wanted Joe because he told me a few times that Joe would never miss a particular item. He was referring to some peppers that we had on sale that week. We had run out because the replacement peppers were rejected from the warehouse due to inferior quality. I showed him the out-of-stock sheet, but he refused to accept it. That's when I really knew he was trying to push me out.

I decided to hand in my two weeks' notice. I was off for the next two days but when I returned, I was told that my district manager, the produce merchandiser, and a hand full of store directors had been trying to contact me. I did not answer any of their calls, I was so upset that tears came into my eyes.

I had done so much for the company and now I was being pushed out by a store director who I thought was unfair. Unknown to me at the time but my district manager Mr. Bausch had been in the store the day after I turned in my notice. He was overheard talking to Mr. Thorson about my two weeks' notice. He wanted to know why a person with all my experience and that he had been with the company for a long time would want to leave.

Mr. Bausch called and called, and I finally answered. He was such a good person I just couldn't ignore him any longer. He was responsible for me being at the store in the first place. We discussed what had been happening at the store and the situation I was in. I told him Thorson was trying to get rid of me, but to make my leaving look legitimate he was first going to write me up for not having peppers. I told him about the shortage and the out-of-stock sheet.

Mr. Bausch told me that he had been alerted by some people in the human resource department at the home office about something going on at Store #2990. They said Mr. Camacho never had any issues with anyone and they were shocked to see an e-mail from me coming into the H.R. office. I had sent emails to everyone to get their attention and make them aware of what was happening at the location.

He told me he had talked to Mr. Thorson and asked if I would please agree to speak with him and give him a second chance. The next day I returned to the store and Mr. Thorson kindly asked if we could go outside and talk. He immediately apologized and told me that he had been having a difficult time the day he confronted me. He told me that he did not want me to leave.

I figured Mr. Bausch told him that if I left there would be consequences, and it was not going to go well for him. I decided to stay, and relations between us got much better. Before long everything that happened was a distant memory and our friendship was restored like it had been when I used to help out his produce department down the street.

So, every time Mr. Bausch came in and saw that everyone was getting along, including us, it made him happy. Knowing good attitudes created a better working environment, Mr. Bausch always wanted to see everyone getting along.

COVID-19

Wednesday, February 12, 2019, was a day I will not easily forget. I went to the store early to prepare an advertisement, put together the salad wall, and place some orders. I also got my shingles vaccine.

Cut fruit and salad wall

I wanted to get everything done because I was scheduled to be off Thursday and Friday and wasn't going to return until Saturday. That evening around six or seven o'clock my phone blew up ringing and ringing. I always ignored calls on my days off, but I felt like something was very wrong because my store director never called that many times.

The next morning, I returned his call, and he asked, "Have you heard the news?"

I responded, "I just woke up and saw that you had called."

"You need to get back to the store as soon as possible. There has been a major virus outbreak, and we need to figure out what to do."

Stack It High - see it fly

Potatoe and onion table

Taking a break   *The leaf section store #3522*

Mike Newman's Best in Class wet-rack set store #3522 *Mike Newman's work*

Re-Grand ready at #3522 *Jeremy Morris, Produce Merchandizer, giving me detailed instructions*

I thought the world must be coming to an end.

When I got to the store, it was a mad house. Everyone was in a panic and stocking up on food, canned goods, and anything else they could get their hands on. The atmosphere was insane.

It was the beginning of the Covid-19 Pandemic. Covid stood for the coronavirus. Nineteen because the virus was first discovered by a scientist in China in 2019. At first, it sounded like a rumor and not too many people were taking it seriously. Then people started getting extremely ill and some died. It wasn't long before the virus spread like crazy all over the world. Italy was the first to be badly impacted, and about two weeks later the virus showed up in the United States. The government was scrambling to try to figure out how to deal with and contain the virus.

We learned that it was passed from person to person, but not airborne and that we were required to wear masks over our noses and mouth to stop the spread. Everyone was being instructed to stay inside and shelter in place. We were only to go outside to get essentials to live on. Some states decided that grocery stores and a few other specific businesses were deemed essential and would be allowed to stay open. All other businesses were required to close their doors.

My work

Holiday ready

Wet-rack

Just being me

At the store I worked several days in a row and logged for about eighty to ninety hours per week. Overtime was approved right away because we needed people to staff the store. However, everyone was scared and did not want to leave their home. We found out that elderly people were the most at risk, but many younger people didn't want to take a risk and embraced working from home.

THE UPS AND DOWNS OF J.C.

Summertime favorites

The tomato table

At work

Store #2990 PRIDE

There would be terrible consequences for businesses and many changes would happen in the food industry as a result of the outbreak. Lives were changed drastically, with many suffering from anxiety and depression. The suicide rate rose during the pandemic. Although everyone was being incredibly careful, the virus ended up killing thousands.

The pharmaceutical companies were tasked with finding a cure and quickly started promoting vaccines. Of course, everyone was skeptical because the companies had not had enough time to test the vaccines. The government issued a mandate stating that everyone had to be tested and vaccinated.

The nut table

Many people were already thinking our government was behind the viral outbreak in an attempt to downsize humanity. Now they were afraid of taking the vaccine because they didn't think our government could be trusted.

Re-setting the juice and salad wall

Summer sets

Each day when I returned home from work, I entered the house through the garage, took off my clothes, and washed them. If I had been exposed, I did not want to give the virus to my mother. With her being up in age, the disease would have been fatal to her.

Even though there wasn't enough proof the vaccines would work, I was one of the first to take the Moderna Clinical Trial vaccines. I did not want to put my mother in her grave before her time.

THE PANDEMIC

At work, I was feeling terrible the first couple of days, and they thought I might have the virus. I was sent home and told I could not come back unless I tested negative. Fortunately, the test came back negative and when I informed Tom Thumb that I had participated in the Moderna Clinical Trials, they allowed me to return to work.

Frankie and his amazing work

THE UPS AND DOWNS OF J.C.

It's cold outside

Frankie selling dipped srawberries

Our driving privileges were restricted. We were supposed to carry a piece of paper showing we had permission to go to work. Everyone else was forced to work from home. No large gatherings were allowed so people mostly kept to themselves. Business meetings, school classes, and ceremonies of any kind were held online.

Empty shelves store #2990

The pandemic experience

Ordering the goods

More deliveries

At our store, the pandemic brought all of us closer to each other; we were like a big family. Mr. Thorson allowed us to get our food and other products before customers arrived. He also had the deli department make pizzas and sandwiches for everyone working at the store. He continually thanked all of us for helping out each day.

Summer sets

The produce department, "Standing Tall"

Cut fruit endcap

Eventually, more vaccines were produced to help protect people, and in May 2023 the government claimed the deadly virus had been contained. We learned to work and live with the virus and were instructed to get an occasional shot similar to a FLU shot. Slowly, life returned to normal.

Massive panic at store #2990

THE UPS AND DOWNS OF J.C.

Long lines and everyone stocking up

Top three managers - David Williams, Arthur Smith, and Brian Jones

LIVE OAK

A new store #3311 was being built in downtown Dallas on Live Oak Steet, and I was talked into joining the opening team. The company was not too sure about opening the store with the current situation that had just happened in the country.

Live Oak promo set

Live Oak fruit and promo set

Front promo display store #store #3311

Super Bowl display

The store was nice and had underground parking that was intended to keep customers cool in the summer and warm in the winter. Initially, I liked the store and had fun working there. I knew everything about the store and where everything was located. Just like Mr. Bausch had told me many times before, at the time, I thought the location was right for me.

Grand Opening store #store #3311

In the beginning store #store #3311

Empty shelves and equipment

Much better

During a bad winter storm our power was knocked out, and the store did not have a generator. We lost a lot of our inventory, so after the storm I spoke to our District Manager, Mr. Bausch. I said, "We need to install a generator. If we would have had a generator, we would have been the only store in the area open and ready for business, we could have generated a lot in sales."

The Citrus Table

The Organic Table

Front view of store #3311

My Crew at store store #3311

My name badge store store #3311

Some familiar co-wokers store store #3311

Setting some shelves

The rest of the crew store #3311

Store at Live Oak and Texas Street

Almost complete

I already had gone through an adventurous experience at Store #2990, when we had a power outage and had to pull everything off the shelves. We boxed up what we could salvage and put the boxes into the back cooler. We had to dispose of some items but saved most of our stock. I also helped other stores with their inventory, re-grands, or simple re-sets. The generator at the store allowed us to salvage most of our stock and remain open for business.

Panic at store #2990

    The crew I had at the new location was decent but there were a number of issues I had to deal with. I had been looking for a wet-rack set-up person. A man came to the store and interviewed with me. He told me that he could set the wet rack in two hours. I told him, "If you can set it in four hours, I will be happy." I thought I had found the right person, so I hired him.

    He struggled with that wet rack so many times I almost felt sorry for him. Oftentimes he would tell me he just wasn't feeling good. On one shift he cut himself badly with a knife and then started missing work. He had some serious issues. One day, he told another employee to call 911 and let them know he was having a heart attack. The fire department sent an ambulance along with a full medical staff to the store. After thoroughly checking him, one of the medics said, "There is nothing wrong with you." When they questioned him and learned that he was just experiencing a fast heat rate we sent him home.

Store #3311 under construction

After about ten months, I requested a transfer. The business at the store was not what I had been expecting; it was terribly slow for me. I was used to working hard and running around from one table to another. I was able to return to my original Store #2990 where I was named the trainer for the district.

Pack and full on aisle #11

Pistachios display

Summertime favorites

Re-set complete

MY WONDERFUL FATHER

When I returned to the store, Mr. Thorson was no longer there. Mr. Jones had been named the Store Director, and he had a distinctive style of getting things done. His methods were not bad, but he could be pushy at times. We got along most of the time, but had a few run-ins.

I decided to take a few days off and go visit my dad. I took him out to eat at his favorite restaurant, Cuquita's that served Mexican food. We sat, ate fajitas, and talked about many things. I was able to share my story how God had changed my life forever in 1996.

Taking our Dad out to eat

My Father at his favorite resturant, Cuquita's

A picture of my wonderful Father

My Father's favorite resturant

Telling my dad the story that day brought tears to my eyes because I was living proof that people could change. He was happy for me and had seen the change in me. He thanked me for coming to visit and spending time with him.

JORGE A. CAMACHO

Visiting my wonderful Father

Even though I worked lots of days, nights, and many hours I still made it a priority to either call or visit him. I owed him my life in many ways and wanted to be there for him. So, visiting him and taking him out to eat made his day and my day. He was a wonderful father!

Taco time at my Dad's

Dad and Romeo

Dad, my older brother "Beto", and me

Family gathering

My Father and some of his grandkids

Father, Alma, Josh, and Jacob

Father and my two sisters Alma & Mary

Happy 90th birthday Dad

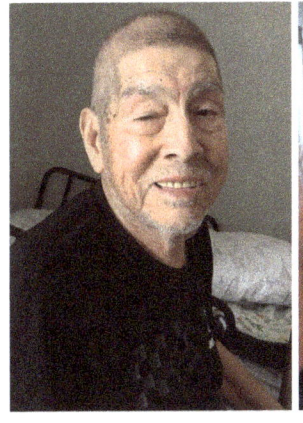 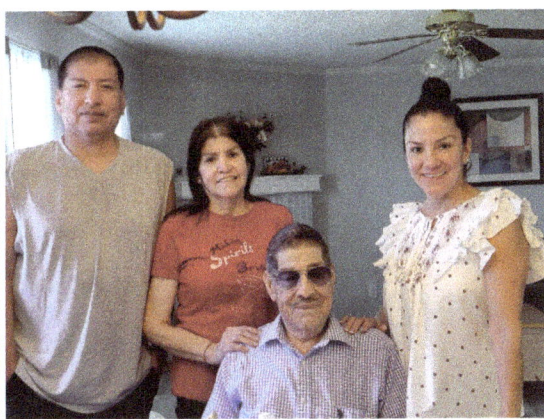

My wonderful Father 94 years   *Visiting our Dad 2023*

The next day might have been like any other, but after spending time with my dad, I had a blessed feeling. Being sober and not having to deal with the headaches that came after a night of heavy drinking was fantastic. Most importantly I was alive. I decided to go to an AA meeting in hopes of telling my story.

God is faithful and I was able to encourage a person named Robert about how God would change his life if he would let Him. I let him know he would be surprised by how his friends and family would be impacted if he were willing to change. Lastly, I told him, "Keep coming back to the meetings and work your program because you are worthy. That's how I started out when God first touched me. The rest will be up to Him."

MY MEMORIES OF LIFES UPS AND DOWNS AND SOME PLEASURES

J.F.K - TOLLING OF THE BELLS

November 22, 2013, was a cold, gray, and wet day. It was the 50th Anniversary of JFK's assassination, and the tolling of the bells in Dallas, Texas was heard across the city.

The day Kennedy was assassinated was a sad day for our Nation. I was only a year old when the event happened, and it made me sad and caused me to cry like many did on that fateful day. I was watching the ceremony on television and waiting with anticipation to hear him speak. A speech that was never heard on that terrible day.

JORGE A. CAMACHO

J.F.K.

American flag

The following is an excerpt from JFK's speech he had prepared for delivery at the Trade Mart in Dallas, Texas.

> ...We in this country, in this generation, are – by destiny rather than choice – the watchmen on the walls of world freedom. We ask, therefore, that we may be worthy of our power and responsibility, that we may exercise our strength with wisdom and restraint, and that we may achieve in our time and for all time the ancient vision of "peace on earth, good will toward men." That must always be our goal, and the righteousness of our cause must always underlie our strength. For as was written long ago: "except the Lord keep the city, the watchman waketh but in vain." (https://www.jfklibrary.org/archives/other-resources/john-f-kennedy-speeches/dallas-tx-trade-mart-undelivered-19631122)

He was a President who at the time represented the great hope that was to come. His memory lives on in all of our hearts.

J.F.K.

THE CONTROVERSIAL CALL

In 2013 the Cowboys were 4 and 4 in and could have easily been 7 and 1. But they had a tough game here and there and couldn't get it done. They had a shoot-out with the Denver Broncos but ended up losing. On October 27, 2013, they were up 30 to 24 against the Detroit Lions with less than a minute to play, but Detroit executed a drive and scored, what a heartbreaker.

Tony Romo needed to take a lesson from the Dallas Mavericks who got it together and won it all in 2011. They beat the best teams in the N.B.A., winning the finals in six games. Boy that was something. Especially considering they were the underdogs in every series. Romo was going to have to win the close games to prove he had what it took to be the best.

I was a Cowboy fan for life and always had faith that they were going to be great. My team still had a chance, a chance for our quarterback to prove to everyone he was a top-rated passer.

Then the walls came crashing down. In 2014 the Cowboys were picked to go 4 and 12 or 5 and 11. After losing to the San Franciso 49ers, they won their next six games. They had one of the best offensive lines in football. They beat the former Super Bowl Champs, the Seattle Seahawks 30 to 23, in their house and at their own game.

They finished season 12 and 4 and were undefeated on the road. They were Road Warriors. In round one they played the Detroit Lions, and it was a remarkably close game, but unlike the 2013 season they prevailed winning 24 to 20.

Next came round two which was the NFC Divisional playoff game against the Green Bay Packers. The game had been close all day and the score was 26 to 21. The cowboys marched down the field with precision. They had the first down but on the next two plays Green Bay held them, now it was third down. Romo passed to Cole Beasly who caught the ball at the thirty-five but landed at the 32-yard line a foot and half shy of a first down. On fourth down Dez Bryant lined up wide left. Tony Romo took the snap, dropped back, and saw Bryant open down the sideline. Tony threw a perfect pass right into his arms. Dez took off and as the defender tackled him, he extended his arms over the goal line. When he fell to the ground the ball popped up a few inches, but from the replay it looked like the ball never left his control.

The controversial call

First and goal

I knew they were going to score which would send them to the N.F.C. title game against the Seattle Seahawks, a team they had already beaten with their strong running attack. Then it happened…Green Bay threw the challenge flag, and the refs overturned the call. The Boys lost 26 to 21, but in my mind, they should have won that game.

I had been caught up in all the hype and excitement thinking they were Super Bowl bound. I went to Sports Academy and bought all kinds of Cowboys gear. Everyone in Dallas/Ft. Worth was excited and needed them to be successful that year to show the world how good they really were.

That season was one heck of a ride, and I had a seat. I was so saddened, especially for Tony Romo and Jason Witten. So close and a chance to win it all. I cried out, "No… No… No, how could this be happening?" I would have to wait for another season.

Romo and Witten should have already won two Super Bowls. The missed fumble in 2007 spoiled their season and now the controversial call spoiled their 2014 season.

HEARTBREAK

I usually attended my son's football games without telling him so he wouldn't be nervous. I would sneak up into the stands and watch the games, which were entertaining. But mostly I attended to see Justin perform in the band. I took a lot of pictures of my precious son. He was growing up right before my very eyes.

He had this wonderful girl in his life. She was incredibly supportive of him in many ways and encouraged him to make sure his homework was done. They would go out to a restaurant, a movie, or just hang out. They were having a lot of fun. I was disappointed at first but seeing him happy made me happy for both of them. I was glad that he had someone to whom he could relate. I thought, "What a beautiful thing!"

She stayed with us a few days during a winter storm that had shut down a lot of places. No one was out on the streets. That's when Justin suddenly decided to end their relationship and apparently for no good reason. At first, I thought he was just playing, but he was not. I did not think his timing was very good and felt she deserved to be treated better.

We were all saddened and heartbroken, especially my mother. I could not believe it myself. It affected us all in many ways. As we got to know her, she became part of the family. We all liked her and thought she was a great person,

My wonderful Mother and me

My beautiful Mother

Mother and my sister Mary

Mary and Whitney 2002

Mary, Matthew, and Whitney Williams

I told my son to really think about what he was doing and encouraged him to go back to her. My suggestion was more for the family so it would stop the pain we were all enduring. He said he did not want to do something dumb or stupid, and he didn't want to hurt her. He had hurt her before and did not want to feel guilty. He said he still cared and had feelings for her, but just wanted to be single.

He also told her that there was not another girl involved and that he would still be there for her, but only as a friend. But she desired more than just friendship.

I felt her pain because the same thing had happened to me twice. All I could do was offer advice and encourage her to stay focused on school. I told her that the pain would go away over time, and she would find someone else one day.

Later my son shared that she was trying to tie him down, and he did not want to be tied down. He was too young and wanted to enjoy his young life. I had to agree and asked why he had not told me this before.

Their relationship lasted about two years, and they remained friends. Neither of them harbored any resentment whatsoever and we let her know that she was more than welcome to visit anytime. Of course, we had no idea at the time that he would meet the love of his life, Trista. More on that later.

First date

REFLECTIONS

Like father, like son, Justin started working for Tom Thumb. As always, I was proud of him. He was doing a wonderful job and liked what he was doing.

Unfortunately, his store manager was a jerk. He was rude to his employees and had no clue how to treat people. After a year, Justin couldn't take it anymore and walked out. Everyone was shocked. The manager called my store and asked to speak with me. He apologized and begged me to talk to Justin. He said, "Please tell him to come back."

I spoke to Justin about what happened and encouraged him to go back, finish out the week, and leave in good standing. Justin took the high road and did as I suggested. He showed what an incredible young man he was.

Not long after his attitude caught up with him, the so-called manager was demoted and sent far away as punishment. Apparently, others started complaining about him and he eventually quit.

My son is a great person, extremely outgoing and enjoys collaborating with people. He has excellent people skills. Target hired him, and they like having him on their team. I know that it will only be a matter of time before he moves up the ladder and continues to be successful.

MOCHA

One day Justin asked me for a pet dog. I told him that it was a big responsibility to own a dog. Of course, like most kids would, he asked me, "Why."

I responded, "Because I have had a few in the past. You have to give them lots of attention and love them all the time. The saddest part is when it is time for them to go, it hurts so much because they had become part of the family. I have lost some dogs in unusual ways and felt the pain."

Well, after a while, he took matters in his own hands. He decided to get a dog and surprise the heck out of me and Mother. He told us, "Since you would not get me one, I decided to get one by myself."

THE UPS AND DOWNS OF J.C.

Mocha having fun 2022

Mocha relaxing 2022

Mocha outside 2020

He had always wanted a German Sheppard and located a dog breeder. When he got to the breeder's place, he saw five or six puppies huddling together. He was looking for a male dog, but out of all the pups only one came up to him. It was a female which is not bad.

He told the breeder, "I'll take that one, since it likes me."

He wanted to name her Bear, but I told him that was a male name. So, we agreed on Mocha, which was a wonderful name for a female dog.

We raised her inside and she was getting aggressive at times, so we sent her to obedience school. She turned out fine and did she love Justin. She also protected my wonderful mother, Rosa, with her life.

Christmas 2022

Mother, Mocha, and me 2017

In 2018, Mother, Justin, myself, and, of course, Mocha moved to Carrollton, Texas. Justin lived with us for about two years before deciding to move out and get an apartment on his own. He was dating a girl named Trista and Mocha didn't seem to like her at the time. Trista was afraid of her as well.

Mocha and me 2019

Our precious pet Mocha 2019

Justin was afraid she might end up biting her so not wanting to take a chance he left Mocha with us. We always knew when Justin would come over, because Mocha would go to the front window and start barking, being the smart dog that she is.

THE PROPOSAL, WEDDING BELLS, & IT'S A GIRL

Approximately two years after Justin moved out, he told us that he planned to propose to Trista at Reunion Tower. On January 23, 2021, Trista's family and our family were present when Justin asked her to be his wife. What a beautiful moment for all of us to experience.

Justin's proposal January 23, 2021

Doug, Trista, Justin, and Jenny

 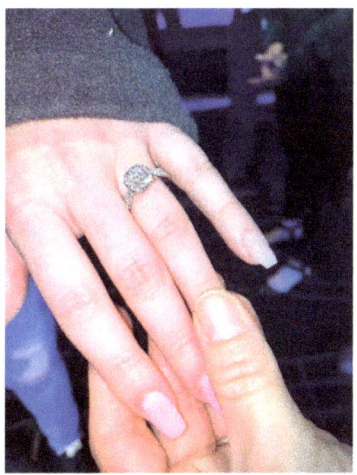

Justin and Trista 2021 *Trista's engagement ring 2021*

Justin, Trista, Mother, and me 2021 *Mary, Justin, Trista, Mother, and me 2021*

Trista, Justin, and Madison 2021

Lily, Trista, Robert, and Austin 2021

The Proposal Cheers 2021

Engagement Party 2021

Kissing in the rain 2021

Trista's best friend Lindsay 2021

Holding hands in the city 2021

Engaged - Justin and Trista 2021

Justin and Trista

The wedding bells tolled, and on April 16, 2022, they became husband and wife.

*The wedding
April, 16 2022*

Jenny and Trista before the wedding

Justin walking to the wedding altar

Henry, Justin's best man

Justin Adam and his bridesmen

Justin, Paul, and Matthew

High in the air

Bridesmaids before the wedding

Trista and her cousin Kirstyn

Trista and Madison

The Bridesmaids

Justin's tears of joy

Justin and Trista - Just Married

Justin escorting Trista off the carriage

One more kiss for the ages

Coming down the stairs at the wedding reception

Cutting the cake

Justin and Trista with the donkeys

Bob Finch at the reception

Jenny, Justin, and Trista

Doug, Jenny, Justin, Trista, Robert, Austin, and Lily

Mary, Justin, Trista, and Me

Father, Justin, Trista, and Mother

Mother, Justin, Trista, and Tia Amelia

Jacob, Alma, Justin, Trista, Joel, and Josh

Celina, Justin, Trista, Elsa, and Alex

Cameron, Cheri, Justin, Trista, Pete, and Ciera

Chuck's wife, Justin, Trista, and Chuck Self

Madison, Justin, Trista, and Matthew

Shanda, Justin, Trista, J.J., and my brother Pepe

Kirstyn, Lacy, Justin, Trista, Gavin, and Barrett

Jenny, Justin, Trista, and Robert

Jenny, Justin, Trista, and Doug

Alma, Justin, Trista, and Joel

Cameron, Justin, and Gavin

Doug and Jenny

Whitney and Mary C. Williams

Barrett, Gavin, Lacy, and Kirstyn

Nuno and Roxy at the reception

My little brother Pepe, Father, Justin, Trista, Beto, and me

"Cowboy" and his beautiful family

Gavin and Cameron

My older brother and his wife

They purchased a piece of land in Melissa, Texas, where they planned to build their dream house. They designed the home themselves and had it built. The home was beautiful, and they moved in with their two incredible dogs, Nico, and Sky.

SOLD to Justin and Trista   *The Camacho's residence being built in Melissa, Texas 2022*

Progressing little by little

Stonework and brick being installed

The grass and landsacpe complete

Garage almost complete

Wow a new home in Melissa, Texas

Justin, Nico, and Sky on the staircase

Nico and Sky taking a break

The only thing missing in their lives was a child. In March 2022 they let Trista's parents, and our side of the family know they were expecting. They wanted to surprise other family members and friends by throwing a party at Top Golf. Everyone was excited when they announced that Trista was expecting. Justin stepped up to hit a ball but before swinging he said, "When the ball lands everything will either turn pink if it is a girl or blue if it is a boy.

2023 gender reveal party - It's a Girl

Justin, Trista, and Mother   *Jenny, Justin, Trista, and Doug*

Camacho and Williams Families   *Henry, Trista, and Justin*

Ryan, Jess, Trista, and Justin   *Lindsay, Trista, and Justin*

It wasn't long before Tayln Rose Camacho came into the world. On November 3, 2023, Trista gave birth to a beautiful baby girl twenty inches long and weighing seven pounds and eight ounces. Their lives were forever changed.

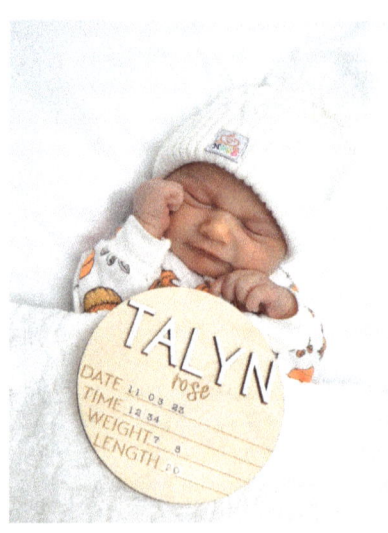 

The Birth of Talyn Rose Camacho   *Trista, Talyn, and Justin*
November 3, 2023

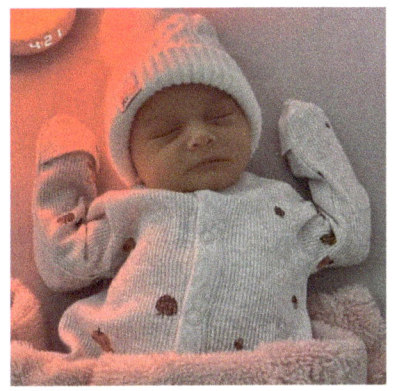

Talyn's second day *Talyn Rose Camacho*

Trista and the Princess *Justin, Talyn, and Trista at the company Christmas party*

Talyn's first Christmas

Justin, Robert, Lily, Trista, and Talyn 2024

Trista and Talyn

MY CUSTOMERS

I always enjoyed talking with our customers, they are so down to earth, and great human beings.

Mr. Richards, a former nose tackle for the San Diego Chargers shopped at our store more than anyone else. He graduated and played ball at S.M.U. where he was named All-American. Though he has been long retired from football he looked like he could still play. Standing at about six foot eight inches tall he was amazingly big and appeared to be healthy. When he saw me, he would come up and greet me or shake my hand; what an impressive person.

Troy Aikman, the former Cowboys quarterback used to come in on occasion and seemed to always be in a hurry. But he would talk to you regardless. Mr. Lane, my Boss took a selfie with him one time. Troy always bought roses for someone special. "Who?" You might be asking; well, it was none of my business. He drove a souped-up JEEP which was genuinely nice and sporty looking.

Tony Romo, another Cowboy quarterback used to come into the store in the evening. He would wear his baseball cap, and some people didn't recognize him. You could not see his eyes. But I could always tell it was him, mainly because of the way he was built. He was also a truly kind, and down-to-earth person.

Another person I have always admired was the NFL All-Time leading rusher in Football, Emmitt Smith. Whenever he was in the store and saw me, he would come over and give me a fist bump and then open and offer his hand. He is a very amazing and outgoing person. I took a picture with him at the store one afternoon.

Occasionally I would see star infielders for the Texas Rangers, Adrian Beltré and Michael *Young*. Both are legends and incredible people. When they saw you, they would greet or shake your hand. Both were very down-to-earth.

Let me tell you about another native Texan, Clayton Kershaw, who grew up and lived in Highland Park until he became a famous Los Angeles Dodger. He still has a home in the area, and his wife is always doing things for the community. I talked to him once and asked if he was that famous pitcher that plays for the Dodgers. He replied, "I am not famous but, I do a little pitching for a team out in California."

I thought, "WOW," what an amazing human being and down to earth person. I always admired those kinds of people. Their family helps the needy and participates with many organizations to fight hunger around the world. I hear his wife does the most, but he gets involved during the off season.

Mr. Babe Laufenberg used to come and shop at my location. I usually only saw him on Saturday or Monday because he was too involved in broadcasting, especially during football season. At one time he was the back-up quarterback for Troy Aikman but was only with the Cowboys for a brief time. He became an announcer for KTVT, one of the area's local television stations. He would come up and greet you as well, he was another great individual.

I would also see the Defensive Coordinator for the Highland Park Scots shopping with his young daughter. The Scotts always have an incredibly good football team, and they don't lose many games.

Heck their Head Coach, Randy Allen, always reminded me of Mr. Tom Landry. He wore the same kind of hat that Mr. Landry wore. His team is always in the playoffs. They have won many State Title's with Randy as their coach. One year he tried to retire, but they convinced him to stay. He is an amazing coach with so much history and is well respected throughout Texas.

I saw our top officials who shopped at the store. Our location was extremely popular and very convenient to the surrounding neighborhood.

SURGERY AT THE HOSPITAL

A lot has happened over the past year.
My Dallas Mavericks were not able to win in the Finals. However, they did an outstanding job going further than anyone expected. I predict they will continue to be good and have a bright future ahead of them.

The Dallas Mavericks

My Texas Rangers won it all in 2023. I was caught up in all the excitement, it was great! They were road warriors and put a number on their opponents. To win that many straight games in a row its unheard of. May not ever happen again. It was their first ever World Series win, and no one can ever take that away from them. They should have won in 2011, but Nelson Cruz mis-judged a ball. They were one out and one strike away from winning it all. But as the old saying goes, "No cigar." That is the way life is sometimes.

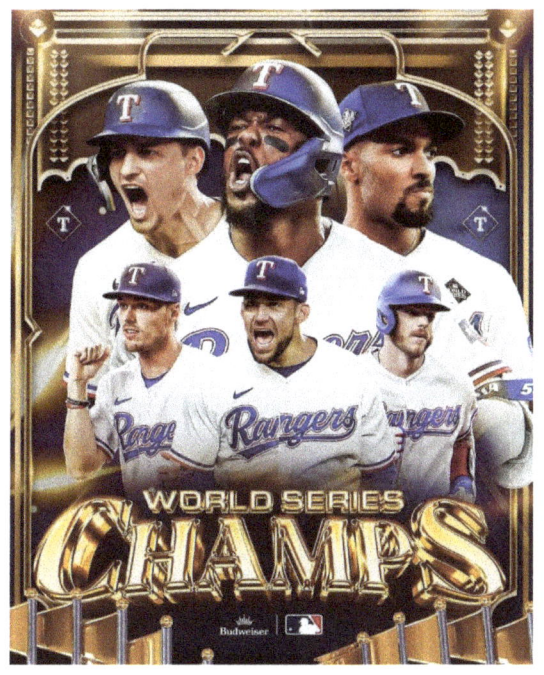

2023 World Series Champs

I lost two of the greatest and most amazing people in my life. My wonderful father and my other father figure, Joe Martinez.

In Loving Memory of my Father   *In Loving Memory of Mr. Joe Martinez*

Putting our Father to rest in 2024

Family gathering after my Father's funeral

My cousin Lolo Camacho and me

I'm standing in between my tia and tio Camacho

My sister, cousin Pedro, Adriana, and me

My family and cousins

My brother Beto, Tia Locha, and Mary

Tia lupe, my Mother, and tia Eufemia Camacho

My Wonderful Family

My other cousins

Mary, Mary Rodriguez, Alma, and Elsa

Family at the funeral

Family picture

I also found out that I had a brain tumor. I underwent surgery on July 3, 2024, to have the tumor removed. I am still recovering at home in Carrollton, Texas with my loving and patient mother.

During surgery I had this dream. In it was a tall mountain that was both awesome and strange. I was floating naked at one end of the mountain and could see the beautiful, green forest on each side, but there was no sun. The mountain was long like a levy and had a road at the very top leading somewhere. The road was narrow, just wide enough for a person to walk on and exceptionally long. I could see some stars or light at the very end. In the distance was a tunnel of some sort with clouds going inside. I believed that the clouds were spirits.

Suddenly, I was awake, but I heard a voice. I could have sworn it was my father saying, "No es tu tiempo. Cuida a tu amá." In english, "It is not your time. Take care of your mom." He was by my side, and I could feel his presence.

The medical team around me was asking how I felt. While they escorted me to a room in ICU unit, they kept asking, "How do you feel. Do you know where you are? What is your name?"

I was seeing a little blurry and was kind of dazed until a few hours later. My family was able to see me again. I am blessed to have such a beautiful, wonderful family that has always been there. They have always been incredibly supportive.

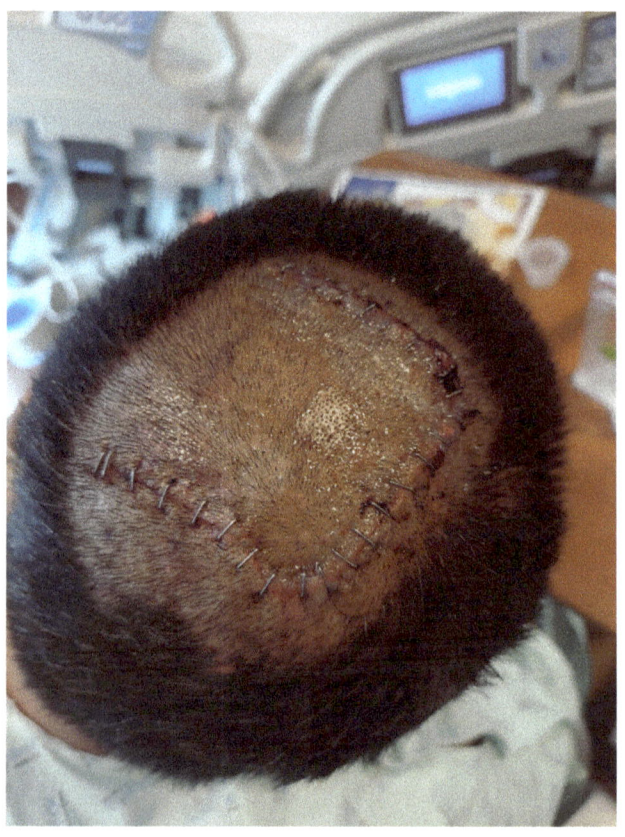

Surgery at the Hospital July 3, 2024

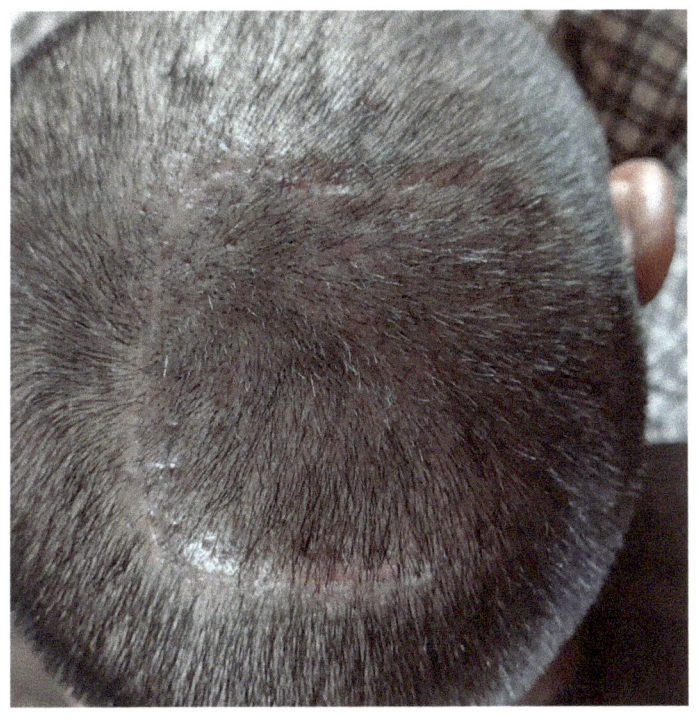

Four months later November 3, 2024

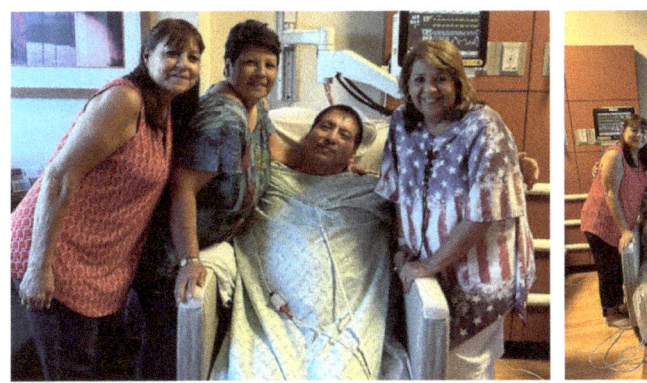 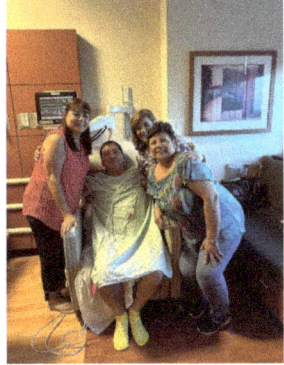

My second family - Sylvia, Josie, Yoli, and Me

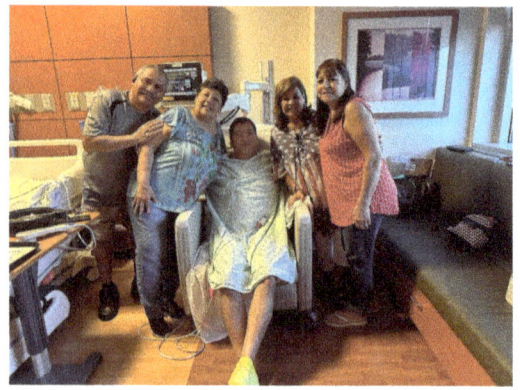 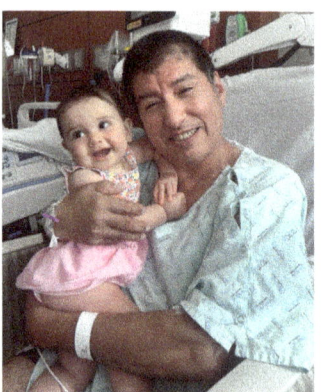

Tony, Josie, Yoli, Sylvia, and me, *My precious little Princess, Talyn Rose*

GIVING THANKS FOR ALL THINGS

I give thanks for all things because I know that GOD is real. I have mentioned it at many of the AA meetings I have attended. I try to keep religion out of my talks because most of the people in recovery do not believe in religion. Most believe in a Higher Power. Let me tell you, the program works if you work it. The program has done wonders for me.

Ledger and me

Madison Williams

Retreat Coordinator /Theology Faculty

B.A., University of Dallas
M.A., Aquinas Institute of Theology

Madison Williams

Trista, Justin, me, Mom, and Nico 2022

Mother and Nico 2022

Me, Beto, Mom, and Tonya at the old home

Happy Thanksgiving 2021

Me, Dad, Mary, Celina, and Elsa

But of all the experiences I have had in life is the one I had at the Glass House, the North Tower of the Lew Sterrett Detention Center, back 1996, for it changed me for all eternity. That is where my spiritual journey began when I heard the voice that was so sincere, so promising, say, "Your time here will pass, and you will be FINE."

I may have left out some events that happened in my past, but not many. Now, the world can read all about my life journey. May God Bless You All.

Justin's new toy 2020 *Premier Event 2022*

My little brother Pepe, Justin Adam, and Mom *Beto, me, Tia Amelia, and Pepe 2005*

Monthly family dinner at Tipico's Restaurant 2024

Flip side View at Tipico's Restaurant

My Father, Justin Adam, and me

My sister Mary, Madison, me and my brother

My Father and his three sons 2022

Cousin Pedrin Sosa, Tia Amelia, and me

Giving thanks for all things 2014

My two amazing sisters, my little brother Pepe, and me

Joel, Alma, Jacob, Beto, Tia Amelia, and me

Trista, Justin, Robert and a friend 2022

Whitney and Mary in the early 1980's

Gerardo, his wife Linda, and Tia Jovita Camacho

Two Brothers - Tio Patricio Sr. and Jesus O. Camacho

Henry and his lovely wife and Virginia Martinez

Another family Dinner at Cuquitas Restaurant

Justin and Trista..Skiing in Colorado

Trista and her father Robert

Lacy, Trista, and Justin with the key to the city

Jenny and Trista

Justin and Trista before the game

Justin Adam Camacho

Family Picture

Madison's graduation

Josh, Miles, and Rose McGuill

Josh and Miles getting ready for a bike ride

Josh, Rose, and baby Miles

Josh and Rose

The Entire Orozco family

The Orozcos

*A Beautiful Picture of Gibert &
Anna and Family*

Gilbert and Anna Orozco

Home sweet home

*Gilbert and Anna Orozco moving
from the Mesquite home*

I wrote this book with hope and prayer for many reasons. I wanted the readers to understand how I have been rescued and blessed in many ways even when I didn't deserve to be blessed or know I was being blessed. I wanted to let you know that a Loving God is always there. He is there for each one of us. He does not sleep while we are sleeping. He and his Angels are always looking after us. That is why we should thank Him every day.

I wanted to let you know how fortunate I am to be here and to be able to share my story. I've shared some good experiences, but mostly bad experiences from my past. My prayer is that those bad experiences will be a warning to you today, especially you young people, about what can happen if you continue to live a fast life without God.

If you are reading this and thinking, "He is nothing more than a hypocrite," you might be right. But one thing no one can deny is the way God has changed my life. I will be sober twenty-eight years on December 6, 2024. I have no one to thank but my Father Almighty.

Ashley and David Rice   *David and Ashley Rice*

Ashley and Daughter   *Ashley and her two beautiful children*

Ashley and Natali   *Ashley Marie Rice*

Ashley and Natali *Ashley and her precious child*

There were times when I thought the State of Texas was punishing me, but all those years they were rescuing me. I had a sense that someone above was looking out after me.

Patty and *Mr. & Mrs. Steele*
Danny Steele

On the road again

I still like the music I grew up with and have attended some concerts to remember how it used to feel. I find myself enjoying the music even more sober. Sometimes, people come up to me and offer me a shot of whiskey or a hit off a joint. I just smile and say, "No thanks," and let them continue with what they think is their "Enjoyment of Life." Back in the day, I used my favorite phrase when responding to a text or a Facebook message about getting high.

Live music with Kat, Big Justin, Matt, and me

Stevie Nicks in concert 2024

Stevie Nicks in concert 2024

However, I learned the hard way that when you continue to make the same mistake all the time eventually the mistake catches up to you and you pay a price. Mine did, and when I went to prison there were probably many people wondering what had happened to me. They had no idea what I had been through and that I had been sent down south to serve a prison sentence for drinking and driving. Not a good place for anyone to end up.

I now realize it is okay to make mistakes, because God will never leave us or forsake us. But you need to always remember that your actions might cause hardship for your family and loved ones. What they will have to go through if you don't change the direction in your own life.

If you are traveling down the destructive path like I was, change direction. Do it for yourself and make those people in your life happy. They will be proud of you. You must be strong and never show weaknesses.

Lastly, I would like to say, being sober will allow you to have and live a wonderful life.

The good life!

IN CLOSING

I plan to be back at work by early November, hopefully sooner. I plan to work another six to eight more years to make sure I get the full retirement package. That is, if my health allows.

I've learned that life is especially important. One day you are here, and the next you are gone. I have seen it too many times. We all see it on the news. Life is so precious and fragile.

Justin still lives in Melissa, Texas with his beautiful wife Trista. Their daughter Talyn Rose Camacho is such an amazing and beautiful granddaughter. Yes, I am a grandpa. They come by or call me once or twice a week.

I am so proud of Justin. He has done well, and God has blessed him with a beautiful family. He now works with my brother-in-law as a field salesperson, which is an excellent job and keeps him busy. If he is not on the phone, he is on the computer going over and beyond to make sure their customers are taken care of. He is at the company's location which is somewhere in Garland, Texas. It is a bigger facility than the previous one where he was before.

Trista has her own business, which keeps her busy as well, not to mention caring for my granddaughter. Her life can be challenging at times, so Justin helps her when he gets off work. Talyn started walking at ten months. She will turn one year old on November 3rd, boy time sure does fly.

I want to thank my entire family, all my relatives, and my close friends who have been so supportive. Also, my co-workers have shown their support. I want to thank my second family, Sylvia Simon, Yoli Martinez, Josie Martinez, Tom Martinez, Tony

(Josie's shadow), Manny Dela Cruz, Bobby Rubio, and his wonderful wife for being so supportive. Also, their wonderful mother Virgina Martinez for her prayers and support.

MISCELLANEOUS PHOTOS

Enjoying life 2005

Justin Adam and Me - White Betty in the background

Justin Adam having fun 2010

Family Picture 2018

Family picture 2016

Justin and Trista

Go Cowboys 2022

Justin and me at his graduation 2016

Enjoying the game

Mom, Justin, and Mary   *Company coming to visit*

Family get together

Father, Mary, and me   *Mother with all her Children 2020*

Our home in Carrollton, Texas 2020   *The kitchen view before the sale in 2018*

My Wall of Fame

Earlier in the book I talked about my concert experiences. If you have thoughts or images from your experiences, I would love for you to share them. Please email me at, jorgecamacho1507@gmail.com

Special thanks to Larry and Judy Luby for all their help laying out preparing this work for publication.